~ All Time ~

FAMILY FAVORITES™

COUNTRY BARBECUE

PUBLICATIONS INTERNATIONAL, LTD.

Pictured on the front cover *(clockwise from top left)*: Chili Tomato Grilled Chicken *(page 74)* and Charcoal Beef Kabobs *(page 46)*.

Pictured on the back cover: Smoke-Cooked Beef Ribs *(page 40)* and Grilled Corn-on-the-Cob *(page 106)*.

Microwave Cooking: Microwave ovens may vary in wattage. The microwave cooking times given in this publication are approximate. Use the cooking times as guidelines and check for doneness before adding more time. Consult manufacturer's instructions for suitable microwave-safe dishes.

— Contents —

— Barbecue Basics —

Cooking over an open fire is the oldest cooking technique known to man. Developed purely in a quest for survival, this ancient art has come a long way since then—new and innovative grilling and flavoring techniques have turned standard backyard fare into cookout cuisine. This tantalizing style of cooking with its mouthwatering aromas offers endless opportunities for both the novice and experienced pro. A simple review of these barbecue basics will ensure success.

Choosing a Grill

Before you choose a grill, consider where you'll be grilling, what you'll be cooking, the seasons when you'll be grilling and the size of your budget.

Portable Grills: These include the familiar hibachi and small picnic grills. Portability and easy storage are their main advantages.

Covered Cooker: Square, rectangular or kettle-shaped, this versatile covered grill lets you roast, steam, smoke or cook whole meals in any season of the year. Draft controls on the lid and base help control the temperature. Closing dampers reduces the heat; opening them increases it. When the grill is covered, heat is reflected off the insides of the grill cooking the food evenly, and without the cover, the coals are hotter since added air circulation promotes their burning.

Gas Grill: Fast starts, accurate heat control, even cooking and year-round use make this the most convenient type of grill. Bottled gas heats a bed of lava rock or ceramic coals—no charcoal is required. Fat from the meat drips onto the lava rocks and produces smoke for a grilled flavor. Wood chips can be used to create the smoky flavor of charcoal.

Fire Building

For safety's sake, make sure the grill is stable, set away from shrubbery, grass and overhangs. Also, make sure the grill vents are not clogged with ashes before starting a fire. NEVER use gasoline or kerosene as a starter. Either one can cause an explosion. To get a sluggish fire going, do not add lighter fluid directly to hot coals. Instead, place two or three coals in a small metal can and add lighter fluid. Then stack them on the previously burning coals with long-handled tongs and light with a match. These coals will restart the fire. Flare-ups blacken food and are a fire hazard; keep a water-filled spray bottle near the grill to quench them. Remember that coals are very hot. Always wear heavy-duty fireproof mitts when cooking and handling grill and tools.

The number of coals required for barbecuing depends on the size and type of grill and the amount of food to be prepared. Strong winds, very cold temperatures or high humidity increase the number of coals needed for a good fire. As a general rule, it takes about 30 coals to grill one pound of meat under optimum weather conditions.

To light a charcoal fire, arrange the coals in a pyramid shape about 20 to 30 minutes prior to cooking. This shape provides ventilation for the coals to catch. To start with lighter fluid, soak coals with $1/2$ cup fluid. Wait one minute for fluid to soak into the coals. Light with a match. To start with an electric or chimney starter, follow the manufacturer's instructions.

When the coals are ready, they will be about 80% ash gray during the day and will glow at night. Spread into a single layer with long-handled tongs. To lower the temperature, spread coals farther apart or raise the grid.

To raise the cooking temperature, either lower the grid or move coals closer together.

Cooking Methods

Direct Cooking: The food is placed on the grid directly over the coals. Make sure there is enough charcoal in a single layer to extend 1 to 2 inches beyond the area of the food. This method is for quick-cooking foods, such as hamburgers, steaks, kabobs and fish.

Indirect Cooking: The food is placed on the grid over a metal or disposable foil drip pan with the coals banked either to one side or on both sides of the pan. This method is for slow-cooking foods, such as large roasts and whole chickens. Some fatty meats also are cooked over indirect heat to eliminate flare-ups.

When barbecuing by indirect cooking for more than 45 minutes, add 4 to 9 coals around the outer edge of the fire just before you begin grilling. When these coals are ready, add them to the center of the fire as needed to maintain a constant temperature.

Flavored Smoke

Flavored smoke from hardwoods and fresh or dried herbs imparts a special flavor to barbecued foods. As a general rule, a little goes a long way. Added flavorings should complement, not overpower, food's natural taste. Always soak wood chunks or chips in water at least 20 minutes before adding to coals so that they smolder and smoke, not burn. Small bundles of fresh or dried herbs soaked in water can also add fragrant flavor when sprinkled over hot coals. Rosemary, oregano and tarragon, for example, can be teamed with wood chips or simply used by themselves for a unique taste.

Only hardwoods or fruitwoods, such as hickory, oak, mesquite, pear or apple should be used. If you chip your own wood, never use softwoods, such as cedar, spruce or pine; these emit resins that are toxic.

Using a Gas Grill

Carefully follow the instructions in your owner's manual for lighting a gas grill. Once the grill is lit, turn on all burners to "high." The grill should be ready to use in about 10 minutes. For direct and indirect cooking, follow the instructions in your owner's manual. Do not use water to quench flare-ups. Close the hood and turn the heat down until flaring subsides.

Although the distinctive smoky flavor of charcoal is missing on a gas grill, wood chips and chunks are great flavor alternatives. Most manufacturers advise against putting these directly on the lava rocks, since ash can clog the gas lines. Simply soak the chips for 20 minutes, drain and place in a disposable foil drip pan. Poke several holes in the bottom and place it directly on the lava rocks. Preheat it with the grill.

Dry Rubs and Marinades

Dry rubs are blends of seasonings and crushed herbs that are rubbed onto meat before grilling. Marinades add flavor and also moisten the surface of the meat to prevent drying out over hot coals. Marinades include an acidic ingredient for tenderizing, such as wine, vinegar or lemon juice, combined with herbs, seasonings and oil. Fish and vegetables do not need tenderizing and should be marinated for only short periods of time. Beef, pork, lamb and chicken should be marinated for a few hours or overnight. For safety, marinate all meats in the refrigerator. Because marinades contain an acid ingredient, marinating should be done in a glass, ceramic or stainless-steel container. The acid can cause a chemical reaction in an aluminum pan. Resealable plastic food storage bags are also great to hold foods as they marinate.

Reserve some of the marinade before adding the meat to use as a baste while the meat is cooking. A marinade drained from meat can also be used as a baste—just be sure to allow the meat to cook on the grill at least 5 minutes after the last application of marinade.

— *Sizzling* —

BURGERS & SANDWICHES

VEGETARIAN BURGERS

½ cup A.1.® Steak Sauce
¼ cup plain yogurt
⅔ cup slivered almonds
⅔ cup PLANTERS® Salted Peanuts
⅔ cup PLANTERS® Sunflower Kernels
½ cup chopped green bell pepper
¼ cup chopped onion
1 clove garlic, minced
1 tablespoon REGINA® Red Wine Vinegar
2 (5-inch) pita breads, halved
4 lettuce leaves
4 tomato slices

In small bowl, combine ¼ cup steak sauce and yogurt; set aside. In food processor or blender, process almonds, peanuts, sunflower kernels, green pepper, onion and garlic until coarsely chopped. With motor running, slowly add remaining ¼ cup steak sauce and vinegar until blended; shape mixture into 4 patties. Grill burgers over medium heat for 1½ minutes on each side or until heated through, turning once. Split open top edge of each pita bread. Layer lettuce, burger, tomato slice and 2 tablespoons prepared sauce in each pita bread half. *Makes 4 servings*

MEXICALI BURGERS

GUACAMOLE
   1 ripe avocado, pitted
   1 tablespoon salsa or picante sauce
   1 teaspoon fresh lime or lemon juice
   ¼ teaspoon garlic salt

BURGERS
   Tortilla chips
   ⅓ cup salsa or picante sauce
   1 pound ground chuck
   3 tablespoons finely chopped cilantro
   2 tablespoons shredded onion
   1 teaspoon ground cumin
   4 slices Monterey Jack or Cheddar cheese
   4 Kaiser rolls or hamburger buns, split
   Lettuce leaves (optional)
   Sliced tomatoes (optional)

1. Prepare grill with rectangular metal or foil drip pan. Bank briquets on either side of drip pan for indirect cooking.

2. Meanwhile, scoop avocado flesh out of shells with large spoon; place in medium bowl. Mash roughly with fork or wooden spoon, leaving avocado slightly chunky.

3. Stir in 1 tablespoon salsa, lime juice and garlic salt. Let stand at room temperature while grilling burgers. Cover; refrigerate if preparing in advance. Bring to room temperature before serving.

4. Place tortilla chips in large resealable plastic food storage bag; seal. Finely crush chips with mallet or rolling pin to measure ⅓ cup.

5. Combine ⅓ cup salsa, beef, tortilla chips, cilantro, onion and cumin in medium bowl. Mix lightly but thoroughly. Shape mixture into four ½-inch-thick burgers, 4 inches in diameter.

6. Place burgers on grid. Grill burgers, on covered grill, over medium coals 8 to 10 minutes for medium or until desired doneness is reached, turning halfway through grilling time.

7. Place 1 slice cheese on each burger to melt during last 1 to 2 minutes of grilling. If desired, place rolls, cut side down, on grid to toast lightly during last 1 to 2 minutes of grilling. Place burgers between rolls; top burgers with Guacamole. Serve with lettuce and tomatoes. *Makes 4 servings*

Mexicali Burger

BURGERS & SANDWICHES

BARBECUED PORK TENDERLOIN SANDWICHES

½ **cup ketchup**
⅓ **cup packed brown sugar**
2 **tablespoons bourbon or whiskey
    (optional)**
1 **tablespoon Worcestershire sauce**
½ **teaspoon dry mustard**
¼ **teaspoon ground red pepper**
1 **clove garlic, minced**
2 **whole pork tenderloins (about ¾ pound
    each), well trimmed**
1 **large red onion, cut into 6 (¼-inch-thick)
    slices**
6 **hoagie rolls or Kaiser rolls, split**

1. Prepare grill. Combine ketchup, sugar, bourbon, Worcestershire sauce, mustard, ground red pepper and garlic in small, heavy saucepan with ovenproof handle; mix well.

2. Set saucepan on one side of grid.* Place tenderloins on center of grid. Grill tenderloins, on uncovered grill, over medium-hot coals 8 minutes. Simmer sauce 5 minutes or until thickened, stirring occasionally.

*If desired, sauce may be prepared on range-top. Combine ketchup, sugar, bourbon, Worcestershire sauce, mustard, ground red pepper and garlic in small saucepan. Bring to a boil over medium-high heat. Reduce heat to low and simmer, uncovered, 5 minutes or until thickened, stirring occasionally.

3. Turn tenderloins with tongs; continue to grill, uncovered, 5 minutes. Add onion slices to grid. Set aside half of sauce; reserve. Brush tenderloins and onion with a portion of remaining sauce.

4. Continue to grill, uncovered, 7 to 10 minutes or until pork is juicy and barely pink in center, brushing with remaining sauce and turning onion and tenderloins halfway through grilling time. (If desired, insert instant-read thermometer** into center of thickest part of tenderloins. Thermometer should register 160°F.)

5. Carve tenderloins crosswise into thin slices; separate onion slices into rings. Divide meat and onion rings among rolls; drizzle with reserved sauce. *Makes 6 servings*

**Do not leave instant-read thermometer in tenderloins during grilling since the thermometer is not heatproof.

Barbecued Pork Tenderloin Sandwich

AMERICA'S FAVORITE CHEDDAR BEEF BURGERS

1 pound ground beef
⅓ cup A.1.® Steak Sauce, divided
1 medium onion, cut into strips
1 medium green or red bell pepper, cut into strips
1 tablespoon FLEISCHMANN'S® Margarine
4 ounces Cheddar cheese, sliced
4 hamburger rolls
4 tomato slices

In medium bowl, combine ground beef and 3 tablespoons steak sauce; shape mixture into 4 patties. Set aside.

In medium skillet, over medium heat, cook onion and pepper in margarine until tender, stirring occasionally. Stir in remaining steak sauce; keep warm.

Grill burgers over medium heat for 4 minutes on each side or to desired doneness. When almost done, top with cheese; grill until cheese melts. Spoon 2 tablespoons onion mixture onto each roll bottom; top each with burger, tomato slice, some of remaining onion mixture and roll top. Serve immediately. *Makes 4 servings*

GRILLED EGGPLANT SANDWICHES

1 eggplant (about 1¼ pounds)
Salt and black pepper
6 thin slices provolone cheese
6 thin slices deli-style ham or mortadella
Fresh basil leaves (optional)
Olive oil

Cut eggplant into 12 (⅜-inch-thick) rounds; sprinkle both sides with salt and pepper. Top each of 6 eggplant slices with slice of cheese, slice of meat (fold or tear to fit) and a few basil leaves, if desired. Cover with slice of eggplant. Brush one side with olive oil. Secure each sandwich with 2 or 3 toothpicks.

Oil hot grid to help prevent sticking. Grill eggplant, oil side down, on covered grill, over medium KINGSFORD® Briquets, 15 to 20 minutes. Halfway through cooking time, brush top with oil, then turn and continue grilling until eggplant is tender when pierced. (When turning, position sandwiches so toothpicks extend down between spaces in grid.) If eggplant starts to char, move to cooler part of grill. Let sandwiches cool about 5 minutes, then cut into halves or quarters, if desired. Serve warm or at room temperature.
Makes 6 sandwiches

America's Favorite Cheddar Beef Burger

BURGERS & SANDWICHES

ZESTY BURGERS

2 pounds ground beef
½ cup WISH-BONE® Italian Dressing*
2 tablespoons horseradish (optional)
1 carrot, grated
1 medium onion, finely chopped
2 eggs
1 cup plain dry bread crumbs

*Also terrific with Wish-Bone® Robusto Italian Dressing.

In large bowl, combine all ingredients; shape into 6 patties. Grill or broil until burgers are done. Serve, if desired, on hamburger rolls.

Makes 6 servings

TERIYAKI TURKEY BURGERS

1 pound ground turkey
⅓ cup teriyaki sauce
3 tablespoons thinly sliced green onions
¼ cup crushed pineapple, drained
½ teaspoon LAWRY'S® Garlic Powder with Parsley

In medium bowl, combine all ingredients; blend well. Form into 4 patties (mixture will be moist). Grill or broil 5 inches from heat source 3 to 5 minutes on each side or until cooked through.

Makes 4 servings

PRESENTATION: Serve with traditional hamburger trimmings.

MUSHROOM–STUFFED PORK BURGERS

1½ pounds lean ground pork
2 teaspoons butter or margarine
¾ cup thinly sliced fresh mushrooms
¼ cup thinly sliced green onions
1 clove garlic, minced
1 teaspoon Dijon mustard
1 teaspoon Worcestershire sauce
¼ teaspoon salt
⅛ teaspoon black pepper
Hamburger buns (optional)

Prepare grill. Melt butter in small skillet; add mushrooms, onions and garlic. Cook and stir over medium-high heat about 2 minutes or until tender; set aside.

Combine ground pork, mustard, Worcestershire, salt and pepper; mix well. Shape into 12 patties, about 4 inches in diameter. Spoon mushroom mixture onto centers of 6 patties. Spread to within ½ inch of edge. Top with remaining 6 patties; seal edges to enclose filling. Place patties on grid. Grill about 6 inches over medium coals 10 to 15 minutes, turning once. Serve on buns, if desired.

Makes 6 servings

*Favorite recipe from **National Pork Producers Council***

Two–Way Burgers

Grilled Burgers
- **1 pound ground beef**
- **¼ cup minced onion**
- **¼ teaspoon black pepper**

Prepare grill. Combine ground beef, onion and pepper, mixing lightly but thoroughly. Divide beef mixture into 4 equal portions and form into patties 4 inches in diameter. Place patties on grid. Grill over medium coals 10 to 12 minutes or to desired doneness, turning once. Prepare desired recipe and assemble as directed. *Makes 4 beef patties*

TIP: Prepare Grilled Burgers and choose one of two different burger recipes—California Burgers or English Burgers.

California Burgers
- **1 recipe Grilled Burgers (recipe above)**
- **¼ cup plain yogurt**
- **1 teaspoon Dijon mustard**
- **4 whole wheat hamburger buns, split**
- **12 large spinach leaves, stems removed**
- **4 thin slices red onion**
- **4 large mushrooms, sliced**
- **1 small avocado, peeled, seeded and cut into 12 wedges**

Combine yogurt and mustard. On bottom half of each bun, layer equal amount of spinach leaves, onion and mushrooms; top each with Grilled Burger. Arrange 3 avocado wedges on each patty; top with equal amount of yogurt mixture. Close each sandwich with bun top. *Makes 4 servings*

English Burgers
- **1 recipe Grilled Burgers (recipe at left)**
- **¼ cup horseradish sauce**
- **¼ cup chopped tomato**
- **2 tablespoons crumbled crisply cooked bacon***
- **4 English muffins, split and lightly toasted**

*One tablespoon canned real bacon bits may be substituted for cooked bacon.

Combine horseradish sauce, tomato and bacon. Place Grilled Burger on each muffin half. Spoon equal amount of horseradish sauce mixture over each patty. Cover with remaining muffin half.
Makes 4 servings

Favorite recipe from **National Cattlemen's Beef Association**

BRATS 'N' BEER

- **1 can or bottle (12 ounces) beer (not dark)**
- **4 bratwurst (about 1 pound)**
- **1 sweet or Spanish onion, thinly sliced, separated into rings**
- **1 tablespoon olive oil**
- **¼ teaspoon salt**
- **¼ teaspoon ground black pepper**
- **4 hot dog rolls**

Prepare coals for grilling. Pour beer into heavy medium saucepan with ovenproof handle. (If not ovenproof, wrap heavy-duty foil around handle.) Place saucepan on grill. Pierce bratwurst with knife; add to beer. Simmer, uncovered, over medium coals, 15 minutes, turning once.

Place onion rings on heavy-duty foil. Drizzle with oil; sprinkle with salt and pepper. Fold sides of foil over rings to enclose. Place onion slices on grill. Grill, uncovered, 10 to 15 minutes or until onion slices are tender.

Transfer bratwurst to grill. Remove saucepan from grill; discard beer. Grill bratwurst, 10 minutes or until browned and cooked through, turning once. Place bratwurst in rolls. Top each with onion slices. Garnish as desired. *Makes 4 servings*

CHEESY LAMBURGER

- **1 pound lean ground American lamb**
- **¼ cup (1 ounce) shredded Cheddar cheese**
- **2 tablespoons sweet pickle relish**
- **2 tablespoons finely chopped onion**
- **1 tablespoon finely chopped green bell pepper**
- **1 teaspoon Dijon mustard**
- **4 multigrain hamburger buns, toasted**
- **4 lettuce leaves**
- **4 slices tomato**

Prepare grill. Combine cheese, relish, onion, pepper and mustard in small bowl. Shape lamb into 8 thin patties about 4 inches in diameter. Spoon cheese mixture onto centers of 4 patties. Top each with another patty, pressing edges to seal filling inside. Place burgers on grid. Grill 4 inches over medium coals 5 minutes on each side or to desired doneness. Serve on buns with lettuce and tomato. *Makes 4 servings*

VARIATION: Substitute dill pickle relish and Monterey Jack or Swiss cheese for the sweet relish and Cheddar.

Prep Time: 15 minutes
Cook Time: 10 to 15 minutes

*Favorite recipe from **American Lamb Council***

Brat 'n' Beer

SAVORY STUFFED TURKEY BURGERS

 1 pound ground turkey
¼ cup A.1.® BOLD Steak Sauce, divided
¼ cup chopped onion
½ teaspoon dried thyme leaves
¼ teaspoon ground black pepper
½ cup prepared herb bread stuffing
½ cup whole berry cranberry sauce
 4 slices whole wheat bread, toasted
 4 lettuce leaves

In medium bowl, combine turkey, 2 tablespoons steak sauce, onion, thyme and pepper; shape into 8 thin patties. Place 2 tablespoons prepared stuffing in center of each of 4 patties. Top with remaining patties. Seal edges to form 4 patties; set aside.

In small bowl, combine remaining 2 tablespoons steak sauce and cranberry sauce; set aside.

Grill burgers over medium heat 10 minutes on each side or until turkey is no longer pink. Top each bread slice with lettuce leaf and burger. Serve immediately topped with prepared cranberry sauce mixture. *Makes 4 servings*

GRILLED CHICKEN CROISSANT MONTEREY

½ cup A.1.® Steak Sauce, divided
 1 tablespoon olive oil
 1 tablespoon finely chopped parsley
 1 teaspoon dried minced onion
¼ cup mayonnaise
 4 boneless chicken breast halves, gently pounded (about 12 ounces)
 4 slices Muenster cheese (about 3 ounces)
 4 croissants (6×3 inches each), split
 4 lettuce leaves
 1 small avocado, peeled, pitted and sliced
 4 tomato slices

In small bowl, combine ¼ cup steak sauce, oil, parsley and onion; set aside for basting.

In separate bowl, combine remaining ¼ cup steak sauce and mayonnaise; set aside.

Grill chicken over medium heat for 6 minutes or until no longer pink in center, turning and brushing often with basting sauce. Top each chicken breast with cheese slice; grill until cheese melts. (Discard any remaining basting sauce.)

To serve, spread 1 tablespoon reserved steak sauce/mayonnaise mixture on bottom of each croissant; top with lettuce leaf, avocado slices, tomato slice and chicken breast. Spread 1 tablespoon steak sauce/mayonnaise mixture on each chicken breast; top with croissant top. Serve immediately. *Makes 4 servings*

Savory Stuffed Turkey Burger

SOUTHERN BARBECUE SANDWICH

1 pound boneless sirloin or flank steak*
¾ cup FRENCH'S® Worcestershire Sauce, divided
½ cup ketchup
½ cup light molasses
¼ cup FRENCH'S® Classic Yellow® Mustard
2 tablespoons FRANK'S® Original REDHOT® Cayenne Pepper Sauce
½ teaspoon hickory salt
4 sandwich buns, split

*You may substitute 1 pound pork tenderloin for the steak. Follow steps below. Cook pork until meat is juicy and barely pink in center or substitute leftover sliced steak for the grilled steak. Stir into sauce and heat through.

Place steak in large resealable plastic food storage bag. Pour *½ cup* Worcestershire over steak. Seal bag and marinate meat in refrigerator 20 minutes.

To prepare barbecue sauce, combine ketchup, molasses, remaining *¼ cup* Worcestershire, mustard, RedHot® sauce and hickory salt in medium saucepan. Bring to a boil over high heat. Reduce heat to low. Cook 5 minutes until slightly thickened, stirring occasionally. Set aside.

Place steak on grid, discarding marinade. Grill over hot coals 15 minutes, turning once. Remove steak from grid; let stand 5 minutes. Cut steak diagonally into thin slices. Stir meat into barbecue sauce. Cook until heated through, stirring often. Serve steak and sauce in sandwich buns. Garnish as desired. *Makes 4 servings*

Prep Time: 15 minutes
Marinate Time: 20 minutes
Cook Time: 25 minutes

GRILLED SALMON BURGERS

1 pound fresh boneless, skinless salmon
2 tablespoons sliced green onions
1 teaspoon LAWRY'S® Garlic Pepper
½ teaspoon LAWRY'S® Seasoned Salt
2 tablespoons LAWRY'S® Citrus Grill Marinade with Orange Juice

Add all ingredients to food processor. Process on pulse setting until salmon is well minced. Place mixture in medium bowl; blend well. Form into 4 patties. Broil or grill, 4 to 5 inches from heat source, 3 to 4 minutes on each side, or until cooked through. *Makes 4 servings*

PRESENTATION: Serve on warm toasted hamburger buns.

Southern Barbecue Sandwich

BLUE CHEESE BURGERS WITH RED ONIONS

- **2 pounds ground chuck**
- **2 cloves garlic, minced**
- **1 teaspoon salt**
- **½ teaspoon black pepper**
- **4 ounces blue cheese**
- **⅓ cup coarsely chopped walnuts, toasted**
- **1 torpedo (long) red onion *or* 2 small red onions, sliced into ⅜-inch-thick rounds**
- **2 baguettes (each 12 inches long)**
- **Olive or vegetable oil**

Combine beef, garlic, salt and pepper in medium bowl. Shape meat mixture into 12 oval patties. Mash cheese and blend with walnuts in small bowl. Divide cheese mixture equally; place onto centers of 6 meat patties. Top with remaining meat patties; tightly pinch edges together to seal in filling.

Oil hot grid to help prevent sticking. Grill patties and onion, if desired, on covered grill, over medium KINGSFORD® Briquets, 7 to 12 minutes for medium doneness, turning once. Cut baguettes into 4-inch lengths; split each piece and brush cut side with olive oil. Move cooked burgers to edge of grill to keep warm. Grill bread, oil side down, until lightly toasted. Serve burgers on toasted baguettes. Top with onion slices. *Makes 6 servings*

BLACK GOLD BURGERS

- **¾ cup finely chopped onion**
- **6 large cloves garlic, minced (about 3 tablespoons)**
- **2 tablespoons FLEISCHMANN'S® Margarine**
- **1 tablespoon sugar**
- **¾ cup A.1.® BOLD Steak Sauce**
- **1½ pounds ground beef**
- **6 hamburger rolls, split**

In medium skillet, over medium heat, cook and stir onion and garlic in margarine until tender but not brown; stir in sugar. Reduce heat to low; cook for 10 minutes. Stir in steak sauce; keep warm. Shape ground beef into 6 patties. Grill burgers over medium heat 5 minutes on each side or until done. Place burgers on roll bottoms; top each with 3 tablespoons sauce and roll top. Serve immediately; garnish as desired. *Makes 6 servings*

Blue Cheese Burger with Red Onions

Hearty

STICK-TO-THE-RIBS MEATS

SAVORY GRILLED TOURNEDOS

⅓ **cup A.1.® Steak Sauce**
¼ **cup ketchup**
¼ **cup orange marmalade**
2 **tablespoons lemon juice**
2 **tablespoons minced onion**
1 **clove garlic, crushed**
8 **slices bacon (about 5 ounces)**
8 **(4-ounce) beef tenderloin steaks**
   (tournedos), about 1 inch thick
Mushroom halves, radishes and parsley
   sprigs for garnish

In small bowl, blend steak sauce, ketchup, marmalade, lemon juice, onion and garlic; set aside.

Wrap bacon slice around edge of each steak; secure with string or wooden toothpick. Grill steaks over medium-high heat for 10 minutes or to desired doneness, turning occasionally and brushing often with ½ cup prepared sauce. Remove string or toothpicks; serve steaks with remaining sauce. Garnish with mushroom halves, radishes and parsley, if desired. *Makes 8 servings*

STICK-TO-THE-RIBS MEATS

CALYPSO PORK CHOPS

1 ripe medium papaya, peeled, halved
    lengthwise and seeded
1 teaspoon paprika
½ teaspoon dried thyme leaves
¼ teaspoon salt
¼ teaspoon ground allspice
4 center-cut pork loin chops
    (about 1½ pounds), cut ¾ inch thick
5 tablespoons fresh lime juice, divided
2 tablespoons plus 1½ teaspoons seeded,
    chopped jalapeño peppers,* divided
1 tablespoon vegetable oil
1½ teaspoons grated fresh ginger, divided
1 teaspoon sugar
¼ cup finely diced red bell pepper
    Additional chopped jalapeño pepper for
    garnish

*Jalapeño peppers can sting and irritate the skin;
wear rubber gloves when handling peppers and do
not touch eyes. Wash your hands after handling
peppers.

1. Chop papaya flesh into ¼-inch pieces. Chop
enough papaya to measure 1½ cups. Set aside.

2. Combine paprika, thyme, salt and allspice in
small bowl; rub over both sides of pork chops with
fingers. Place chops in large resealable plastic food
storage bag.

3. Combine 3 tablespoons lime juice, 2
tablespoons jalapeños, oil, 1 teaspoon ginger and
sugar in small bowl; pour over chops. Seal bag
tightly, turning to coat. Marinate in refrigerator 1
to 2 hours.

4. Combine papaya, bell pepper, remaining 2
tablespoons lime juice, remaining 1½ teaspoons
jalapeños and remaining ½ teaspoon ginger in
another small bowl; cover and refrigerate until
serving.

5. Prepare grill. Meanwhile, drain chops; discard
marinade. Place chops on grid. Grill chops, on
covered grill, over medium coals 10 to 12 minutes
or until pork is juicy and barely pink in center,
turning halfway through grilling time. Serve chops
topped with papaya mixture. Garnish, if desired.

Makes 4 servings

PESTO BEEF SWIRLS

⅓ cup A.1.® Steak Sauce
¼ cup grated Parmesan cheese
¼ cup pignoli nuts or walnuts
2 tablespoons dried basil leaves
2 cloves garlic
1 (2-pound) beef flank steak, pounded to
    ½-inch thickness

In blender or food processor, blend all ingredients
except steak to a coarse paste; spread over top of
steak. Cut steak across grain into eight 1-inch-
wide strips. Roll up each strip from short edge;
secure with wooden toothpick. Grill over medium
heat for 7 to 8 minutes on each side or to desired
doneness, brushing often with additional steak
sauce. Remove toothpicks; serve immediately.

Makes 8 servings

Calypso Pork Chop

STICK-TO-THE-RIBS MEATS

HOT & SPICY BEEF BACK RIBS

7 pounds beef back ribs (two 3½-pound slabs)
¾ cup water, divided
1 cup ketchup
2 tablespoons lemon juice
1 teaspoon ground cinnamon
1 teaspoon hot pepper sauce
½ to 1 teaspoon crushed red pepper

Place each slab of ribs, meat side down, in center of double-thick rectangle of heavy-duty aluminum foil. Sprinkle 2 tablespoons water over each slab. To form packets, bring 2 long sides of foil together over top of ribs. Fold edges over 3 or 4 times, pressing crease in tightly each time (allow some air space). Flatten foil at 1 short end; crease to form triangle and fold edge over several times toward package, pressing tightly to seal. Repeat procedure on other end. Place packets on grid directly over low to medium coals. Place cover on grill and cook 1½ hours, turning packets every ½ hour.

In small saucepan, combine ketchup, remaining ½ cup water, lemon juice, cinnamon, hot pepper sauce and crushed red pepper. Bring to a boil; reduce heat and cook 10 to 12 minutes. Remove ribs from foil packets. Place on grid over medium coals and grill 30 to 40 minutes, turning and brushing with sauce occasionally. Serve remaining sauce with ribs.   *Makes about 8 servings*

Favorite recipe from **National Cattlemen's Beef Association**

BARBECUED ROUND–UP ROAST

1 (5-pound) beef round tip roast or beef chuck cross rib roast
1 cup chopped onion
1 cup strong black coffee
1 cup orange juice
1 tablespoon dried rosemary
1 tablespoon dried thyme
1 teaspoon ground pepper

Place roast in shallow glass baking dish. Mix together remaining ingredients; pour over roast. Cover; refrigerate, turning occasionally, at least 6 hours, no longer than 48 hours.

Prepare charcoal grill for barbecuing. With tongs, move glowing coals toward outside edge of grill. Place metal drip pan in center of grill. Push coals around sides of drip pan. Place grill rack 6 inches above drip pan.

Cook roast on grill over medium-hot coals, turning every 15 minutes, for 1½ to 2½ hours. Baste occasionally with marinade while cooking. Discard remaining marinade. After 1½ hours, insert meat thermometer into center of roast. The thermometer should register 140°F for rare, 160°F for medium and 170°F for well-done. Remove roast from heat when thermometer registers 5°F below the temperature of desired doneness. Roast will continue to cook after removal from heat. For easier carving, allow roast to stand in warm place 15 to 20 minutes.   *Makes 10 to 12 servings*

Favorite recipe from **California Beef Council**

STICK-TO-THE-RIBS MEATS

GREEK–STYLE LOIN ROAST

- **1 boneless pork loin roast (3 pounds)**
- **¼ cup olive oil**
- **¼ cup lemon juice**
- **1 teaspoon dried oregano leaves, crushed**
- **1 teaspoon salt**
- **1 teaspoon black pepper**
- **6 cloves garlic, minced**
- **Spicy Yogurt Sauce (recipe follows)**

Place pork loin in large resealable plastic food storage bag. Combine all remaining ingredients except Spicy Yogurt Sauce in small bowl; pour over pork. Seal bag and marinate in refrigerator overnight, turning bag occasionally. Meanwhile, prepare Spicy Yogurt Sauce.

Prepare grill with rectangular foil drip pan. Bank briquets on either side of drip pan for indirect cooking. Remove pork, discarding marinade. Place pork on grid over drip pan. Grill, on covered grill, over low coals 1½ hours or to an internal temperature of 155°F. Let rest 10 minutes. (Internal temperature will rise slightly upon standing.) To serve, slice roast thinly and serve with Spicy Yogurt Sauce. *Makes 8 servings*

SPICY YOGURT SAUCE: Combine 1 cup plain yogurt, 1 peeled and chopped cucumber, ¼ cup minced red onion, ½ teaspoon crushed garlic, ½ teaspoon crushed coriander seeds and ¼ teaspoon crushed red pepper in small bowl; blend well. Cover and refrigerate until ready to serve.

*Favorite recipe from **National Pork Producers Council***

LAMB STEAKS CALYPSO

- **2 American lamb center leg steaks (about 2 pounds)**

MARINADE
- **1 cup chicken broth or bouillon**
- **½ cup packed brown sugar**
- **2 tablespoons fresh lime juice**
- **2 tablespoons rum or additional lime juice**
- **1 clove garlic, minced**
- **1 teaspoon grated fresh ginger**
- **½ teaspoon ground cloves**

Combine marinade ingredients in shallow glass dish or large resealable plastic food storage bag. Add steaks. Cover and marinate in refrigerator 2 hours or overnight.

Prepare grill. Drain steaks, reserving marinade. Grill over medium coals 5 to 7 minutes on each side or to desired doneness, brushing occasionally with marinade. (Do not baste during last 5 minutes of grilling.) *Makes 4 servings*

SERVING SUGGESTION: Serve with grilled sweet potatoes and peppers.

Prep Time: 5 minutes
Marinate Time: 2 to 24 hours
Cook Time: 10 to 15 minutes

*Favorite recipe from **American Lamb Council***

STICK-TO-THE-RIBS MEATS

GUADALAJARA BEEF AND SALSA

- 1 bottle (12 ounces) Mexican dark beer*
- ¼ cup soy sauce
- 2 cloves garlic, minced
- 1 teaspoon ground cumin
- 1 teaspoon chili powder
- 1 teaspoon hot pepper sauce
- 4 beef bottom sirloin steaks or boneless strip steaks (4 to 6 ounces each)
- Salt and black pepper
- Red, green and yellow bell peppers, cut lengthwise into quarters, seeded (optional)
- Salsa (recipe follows)
- Flour tortillas (optional)
- Lime wedges

*Substitute any beer for Mexican dark beer.

Combine beer, soy sauce, garlic, cumin, chili powder and hot pepper sauce in large shallow glass dish or large heavy plastic food storage bag. Add beef; cover dish or close bag. Marinate in refrigerator up to 12 hours, turning beef several times. Remove beef from marinade; discard marinade. Season with salt and pepper.

Oil hot grid to help prevent sticking. Grill beef and bell peppers, if desired, on covered grill, over medium KINGSFORD® Briquets, 8 to 12 minutes, turning once. Beef should be of medium doneness and peppers should be tender. Serve with Salsa, tortillas, if desired, and lime.

Makes 4 servings

Salsa

- 2 cups coarsely chopped seeded tomatoes
- 2 green onions with tops, sliced
- 1 clove garlic, minced
- 1 to 2 teaspoons minced seeded jalapeño or serrano chili pepper, fresh or canned
- 1 tablespoon olive or vegetable oil
- 2 to 3 teaspoons lime juice
- 8 to 10 sprigs fresh cilantro, minced (optional)
- ½ teaspoon salt or to taste
- ½ teaspoon sugar or to taste
- ¼ teaspoon black pepper

Combine tomatoes, green onions, garlic, chili pepper, oil and lime juice in medium bowl. Stir in cilantro, if desired.

Season with salt, sugar and black pepper. Adjust seasonings to taste, adding lime juice or chili pepper, if desired. *Makes about 2 cups*

Guadalajara Beef and Salsa

STICK-TO-THE-RIBS MEATS

TIJUANA BLACKENED STEAK

¾ **teaspoon garlic powder**
¾ **teaspoon onion powder**
¾ **teaspoon ground black pepper**
½ **teaspoon ground white pepper**
¼ **teaspoon ground red pepper**
4 **(4- to 6-ounce) beef shell or strip steaks,
  about ½ inch thick**
½ **cup A.1.® Steak Sauce**
¼ **cup FLEISCHMANN'S® Margarine, melted**

In small bowl, combine garlic powder, onion powder and peppers; spread on waxed paper. Coat both sides of steaks with seasoning mixture.

In small bowl, combine steak sauce and margarine. Grill steaks 10 to 15 minutes or until done, turning and brushing often with ¼ cup steak sauce mixture. Serve steaks with remaining steak sauce mixture. *Makes 4 servings*

GRILLED LAMB SHASHLYK WITH MINTED CREAM SAUCE

2 **pounds lean lamb, cut into 1½-inch cubes**
½ **cup SEVEN SEAS® VIVA® Red Wine!
  Vinegar & Oil Reduced Calorie Dressing**
1 **green pepper, cut into 1-inch chunks**
1 **red pepper, cut into 1-inch chunks**
1 **yellow pepper, cut into 1-inch chunks**
1 **small red onion, cut into wedges**
1 **lemon, thinly sliced**
  Minted Cream Sauce (recipe follows)

• Marinate lamb in dressing, covered, in refrigerator several hours or overnight. Remove lamb from marinade; heat marinade thoroughly.

• Prepare coals for grilling.

• Arrange lamb, vegetables and lemon on skewers. Place on greased grill over hot coals (coals will be glowing).

• Grill, uncovered, 4 to 6 minutes on each side or to desired doneness, brushing frequently with reserved marinade. Serve with Minted Cream Sauce. *Makes 8 servings*

Prep Time: 20 minutes plus marinating
Cook Time: 12 minutes

Minted Cream Sauce
1 **(8-ounce) container PHILADELPHIA
  BRAND® Soft Cream Cheese**
½ **cup plain yogurt**
2 **tablespoons chopped fresh mint**
1 **garlic clove, minced**
⅛ **teaspoon black pepper**
  **Additional chopped fresh mint, for
  garnish**

• Combine cream cheese, yogurt, 2 tablespoons mint, garlic and pepper in food processor or blender; process until well blended. Garnish with additional mint leaves, if desired.

STICK-TO-THE-RIBS MEATS

HOT AND SPICY SPARERIBS

1 rack pork spareribs (3 pounds)
2 tablespoons butter or margarine
1 medium onion, finely chopped
2 cloves garlic, minced
1 can (15 ounces) tomato sauce
⅔ cup cider vinegar
⅔ cup packed brown sugar
2 tablespoons chili powder
1 tablespoon prepared mustard
½ teaspoon pepper

Melt butter in large skillet over low heat. Add onion and garlic; cook and stir until tender. Add remaining ingredients, except ribs, and bring to a boil. Reduce heat and simmer 20 minutes, stirring occasionally.

Place large piece of aluminum foil over coals to catch drippings. Baste meaty side of ribs with sauce. Place ribs on grill, meaty side down, about 6 inches above low coals; baste top side. Cover. Cook about 20 minutes; turn ribs and baste. Cook 45 minutes more or until done, basting every 10 to 15 minutes with sauce.   *Makes 3 servings*

Favorite recipe from **National Pork Producers Council**

LONDON BROIL DIJON

2 tablespoons olive or vegetable oil
2 large heads garlic, separated into cloves
**   and peeled**
1 can (14½ ounces) low-salt beef broth
½ cup water
1 sprig fresh oregano or parsley
1½ tablespoons Dijon mustard
2 pounds beef top round steak or London
**   broil (about 1½ inches thick)**
Salt and black pepper

Heat oil in medium saucepan; add garlic and sauté over medium-low heat, stirring frequently, until garlic just starts to brown in spots. Add broth, water and oregano. Simmer until mixture is reduced by about one third. Process broth mixture, in batches, in blender or food processor until smooth. Return to saucepan; whisk in mustard. Set aside. Season meat with salt and pepper.

Oil hot grid to help prevent sticking. Grill beef, in covered grill, over medium-low KINGSFORD® Briquets, 10 to 14 minutes for medium-rare doneness; 12 to 16 minutes for medium doneness, turning once or twice. Let stand 5 minutes before slicing. Cut across grain into thin, diagonal slices. Gently rewarm sauce and serve as accompaniment.
                                        Makes 6 servings

STICK-TO-THE-RIBS MEATS

FAJITAS WITH AVOCADO SALSA

- **1 beef flank steak (1¼ to 1½ pounds)**
- **¼ cup tequila or nonalcoholic beer**
- **3 tablespoons fresh lime juice**
- **1 tablespoon seeded, minced jalapeño pepper***
- **2 large cloves garlic, minced**
- **1 large red bell pepper**
- **1 large green bell pepper**
- **Avocado Salsa (recipe follows)**
- **8 flour tortillas (6- to 7-inch diameter)**
- **4 slices red onion, cut ¼ inch thick**

*Jalapeño peppers can sting and irritate the skin; wear rubber gloves when handling peppers and do not touch eyes. Wash your hands after handling.

Place steak in large resealable plastic food storage bag. Combine tequila, lime juice, jalapeño and garlic in small bowl; pour over steak. Seal bag tightly, turning to coat. Marinate in refrigerator 1 to 4 hours, turning once.

Stand bell peppers on end on cutting board. Cut off sides into 4 lengthwise slices with utility knife. (Cut close to, but not through, stem.) Discard stem and seeds. Rinse inside of peppers under cold running water. Set aside. Prepare grill. Meanwhile, prepare Avocado Salsa. Wrap tortillas in heavy-duty foil. Drain steak; discard marinade. Place steak, bell peppers and onion slices on grid. Grill, on covered grill, over medium-hot coals 14 to 18 minutes for medium or until desired doneness is

reached, turning steak, bell peppers and onion slices halfway through grilling time. Place tortilla packet on grid during last 5 to 7 minutes of grilling; turn halfway through grilling time to heat through.

Transfer steak to carving board. Carve steak across the grain into thin slices. Slice bell peppers into thin strips. Separate onion slices into rings. Divide among tortillas; roll up and top with Avocado Salsa.

Makes 4 servings

Avocado Salsa

- **1 large ripe avocado, halved and pitted**
- **1 large tomato, seeded and diced**
- **3 tablespoons chopped cilantro**
- **1 tablespoon vegetable oil**
- **1 tablespoon fresh lime juice**
- **2 teaspoons minced fresh or drained, bottled jalapeño pepper**
- **1 clove garlic, minced**
- **½ teaspoon salt**

Scoop avocado flesh from shells with large spoon; place on cutting board. Coarsely chop avocado flesh into ½-inch cubes. Transfer to medium bowl. Gently stir in tomato, cilantro, oil, lime juice, jalapeño, garlic and salt until well combined. Let stand at room temperature while grilling steak. Cover; refrigerate if preparing in advance. Bring to room temperature before serving.

Makes about 1½ cups

Fajitas with Avocado Salsa

STICK-TO-THE-RIBS MEATS

HONEY–CITRUS GLAZED VEAL CHOPS

½ teaspoon grated lime peel
3 tablespoons fresh lime juice
2 tablespoons honey
2 teaspoons grated fresh ginger
4 veal rib chops, cut 1 inch thick
    (about 8 ounces each)

Combine lime peel, lime juice, honey and ginger in small bowl. Place veal rib chops in shallow dish just large enough to hold chops. Brush lime mixture liberally over both sides of chops. Marinate in refrigerator, covered, 30 minutes while preparing coals. Remove chops from dish; brush again with any lime mixture remaining in dish. Place chops on grid over medium coals. Grill 12 to 14 minutes, turning once for medium (160°F), or to desired doneness.   *Makes 4 servings*

Favorite recipe from **National Cattlemen's Beef Association**

ONION–MARINATED STEAK

2 large red onions
¾ cup plus 2 tablespoons WISH-BONE®
    Italian Dressing*
1 (2- to 3-pound) boneless sirloin or London
    broil steak

*Also terrific with Wish-Bone® Robusto Italian or Lite Italian Dressing.

Cut 1 onion in half; set aside one half. Chop remaining onion to equal 1½ cups. In blender or food processor, process ¾ cup Italian dressing and chopped onion until puréed.

In large, shallow nonaluminum baking dish or plastic bag, combine steak with dressing-onion marinade. Cover, or close bag, and marinate in refrigerator, turning occasionally, 3 hours or overnight. Remove steak, reserving marinade.

Grill or broil steak, turning and basting frequently with reserved marinade, until steak is done. *Do not brush with marinade during last 5 minutes of cooking.*

Meanwhile, in saucepan, heat remaining 2 tablespoons Italian dressing and cook remaining onion half, cut into thin slices, stirring occasionally, 4 minutes or until tender. Serve over steak.   *Makes 8 servings*

HICKORY SMOKED HAM WITH MAPLE–MUSTARD SAUCE

Hickory chunks or chips for smoking
1 fully cooked boneless ham
    (about 5 pounds)
¾ cup maple syrup
¾ cup spicy brown mustard or Dijon
    mustard

Soak about 4 wood chunks or several handfuls of wood chips in water; drain. If using canned ham, scrape off any gelatin. If using another type of fully cooked ham, such as bone-in shank, trim most of fat, leaving ⅛-inch layer. (The thinner the fat layer, the better the glaze will adhere to ham.)

Arrange low KINGSFORD® Briquets on each side of rectangular metal or foil drip pan. Pour in hot tap water to fill pan half full. Add soaked wood (all the chunks; part of the chips) to fire.

Oil hot grid to help prevent sticking. Place ham on grid directly above drip pan. Grill ham, on covered grill, 20 to 30 minutes per pound, until meat thermometer inserted in thickest part registers 140°F. If grill has thermometer, maintain cooking temperature of about 200°F. For best flavor, cook slowly over low coals, adding a few briquets to both sides of fire every hour, or as necessary, to maintain constant temperature. Add more soaked hickory chips every 20 to 30 minutes.

Meanwhile, prepare Maple-Mustard Sauce by mixing maple syrup and mustard in small bowl; set aside most of syrup mixture to serve as sauce. Brush ham with remaining mixture several times during last 45 minutes of cooking. Let ham stand 10 minutes before slicing. Slice and serve with Maple-Mustard Sauce. *Makes 12 to 15 servings*

NOTE: Most hams available today are fully cooked and need only be heated to a temperature of 140°F. If you buy a partially cooked ham, often labeled "cook before eating," it needs to be cooked to 160°F.

CIDER GLAZED PORK ROAST

1 pork loin roast (4 to 5 pounds), boned and
    tied
½ cup apple cider
¼ cup Dijon-style mustard
¼ cup vegetable oil
¼ cup soy sauce

Insert meat thermometer in center of thickest part of roast. Arrange medium-hot KINGSFORD® Briquets around drip pan. Place roast over drip pan. Cover grill and cook 2½ to 3 hours, or until thermometer registers 170°F, adding more briquets as necessary. Combine apple cider, mustard, oil and soy sauce. Brush roast with cider mixture 3 or 4 times during last 30 minutes of cooking.

Makes 6 servings

STICK-TO-THE-RIBS MEATS

SAUSAGE, PEPPERS & ONIONS WITH GRILLED POLENTA

5 cups canned chicken broth
1 cup Italian polenta or yellow cornmeal
1½ cups cooked fresh corn or thawed frozen corn
2 tablespoons butter or margarine
1 cup (4 ounces) freshly grated Parmesan cheese
6 Italian-style sausages
2 small to medium red onions, sliced into rounds
1 each medium red and green bell pepper, cored, seeded and cut into 1-inch-wide strips
½ cup Marsala or sweet vermouth (optional)
Olive oil

To make polenta, bring chicken broth to a boil in large pot. Add polenta and cook at a gentle boil, stirring frequently, about 30 minutes. If polenta starts to stick and burn bottom of pot, add up to ½ cup water. During last 5 minutes of cooking, stir in corn and butter. Remove from heat; stir in Parmesan cheese. Transfer polenta into greased 13×9-inch baking pan; let cool until firm and set enough to cut. (Polenta can be prepared a day ahead and held in refrigerator.)

Prick each sausage in 4 or 5 places with fork. Place sausages, red onions and bell peppers in large shallow glass dish or large heavy plastic food storage bag. Pour Marsala over food; cover dish or close bag. Marinate in refrigerator up to 4 hours, turning sausages and vegetables several times. (If you don't wish to marinate sausages and vegetables in Marsala, just eliminate this step.)

Oil hot grid to help prevent sticking. Cut polenta into squares, then cut into triangles, if desired. Brush one side with oil. Grill polenta oil side down, on covered grill, over medium KINGSFORD® Briquets, about 4 minutes until lightly toasted. Halfway through cooking time, brush top with oil, then turn and continue grilling. Move polenta to edge of grill to keep warm.

When coals are medium-low, drain sausages and vegetables from wine; discard wine. Grill sausages on covered grill, 15 to 20 minutes until cooked through, turning several times. After sausages have cooked 10 minutes, place vegetables in center of grid. Grill vegetables 10 to 12 minutes until tender, turning once or twice. *Makes 6 servings*

Sausage, Peppers & Onions with Grilled Polenta

STICK-TO-THE-RIBS MEATS

SMOKE–COOKED BEEF RIBS

**Wood chunks or chips for smoking
4 to 6 pounds beef back ribs, cut into slabs
   of 3 to 4 ribs each
Salt and black pepper
1⅓ cups K.C. MASTERPIECE® Barbecue
   Sauce, divided
Beer at room temperature or hot tap water
Grilled corn-on-the-cob (optional)**

Soak 4 wood chunks or several handfuls of wood chips in water; drain. Spread ribs on baking sheet or tray; season with salt and pepper. Brush with half of sauce. Let stand at cool room temperature up to 30 minutes.

Arrange low KINGSFORD® Briquets on each side of rectangular metal or foil drip pan. (Since ribs have been brushed with sauce before cooking, low heat is needed to keep them moist.) Pour in beer to fill pan half full. Add soaked wood (all the chunks; part of chips) to fire.

Oil hot grid to help prevent sticking. Place ribs on grid, meaty side up, directly above drip pan. Smoke-cook ribs, on covered grill, about 1 hour, brushing remaining sauce over ribs 2 or 3 times during cooking. If grill has thermometer, maintain cooking temperature between 250°F to 275°F. Add a few more briquets after 30 minutes, or as necessary, to maintain constant temperature. Add more soaked wood chips every 30 minutes, if necessary. Serve with grilled corn-on-the-cob, if desired. *Makes 4 to 6 servings*

BEEF KABOBS OVER LEMON RICE

**½ pound boneless beef sirloin steak, cut
   into 1-inch cubes
1 small zucchini, sliced
1 small yellow squash, sliced
1 small red bell pepper, cut into squares
1 small onion, cut into chunks
¼ cup Italian dressing
1 cup hot cooked rice
2 teaspoons fresh lemon juice
1 tablespoon snipped fresh parsley
¼ teaspoon seasoned salt**

Combine beef and vegetables in large resealable plastic food storage bag; add dressing. Seal bag and marinate 4 to 6 hours in refrigerator, turning bag occasionally. Thread beef and vegetables alternately onto 4 metal skewers. Grill over medium coals, or broil, 5 to 7 minutes or to desired doneness, turning and basting with remaining marinade. Combine rice and remaining ingredients. Serve kabobs over rice mixture. *Makes 2 servings*

Favorite recipe from **USA Rice Council**

Beef Kabobs over Lemon Rice

STICK-TO-THE-RIBS MEATS

TERIYAKI BUTTERFLIED LAMB

¾ cup KIKKOMAN® Teriyaki Baste & Glaze
1 teaspoon grated orange peel
1 tablespoon orange juice
1 teaspoon TABASCO® pepper sauce
4 cloves garlic, pressed
1 (4-pound) lamb leg, sirloin or shank half, boned and butterflied

Combine teriyaki baste & glaze, orange peel, orange juice, pepper sauce and garlic; set aside. Trim and discard "fell" and excess fat from lamb. Place lamb on grill 5 inches from hot coals; brush lightly with baste & glaze mixture. Cook 40 minutes, or until meat thermometer inserted into thickest part registers 140°F (for rare), or to desired doneness, turning lamb over occasionally and brushing frequently with remaining baste & glaze mixture. (Or, place lamb on rack of broiler pan. Broil 5 inches from heat 20 minutes, brushing occasionally with baste & glaze mixture. Turn lamb over. Broil 20 minutes longer, or until meat thermometer inserted into thickest part registers 140°F [for rare], or to desired doneness, brushing occasionally with remaining baste & glaze mixture.) *Makes 6 to 8 servings*

MUSTARD–GLAZED RIBS

¾ cup beer
½ cup firmly packed dark brown sugar
½ cup spicy brown mustard
3 tablespoons soy sauce
1 tablespoon catsup
¾ teaspoon TABASCO® pepper sauce
½ teaspoon ground cloves
4 pounds pork spareribs or beef baby back ribs

In medium bowl, combine beer, sugar, mustard, soy sauce, catsup, Tabasco® sauce and cloves; mix well. Position grill rack as far from coals as possible. Place ribs on grill over low heat. For pork ribs, grill 45 minutes; turn occasionally. Brush with mustard glaze. Grill 30 minutes longer or until meat is cooked through; turn and baste ribs often with mustard glaze. (For beef baby back ribs, grill 15 minutes. Brush with mustard glaze. Grill 30 minutes longer or until meat is cooked to desired doneness; turn and baste ribs often with mustard glaze.) Heat any remaining glaze to a boil; serve with ribs. *Makes 4 servings*

STICK-TO-THE-RIBS MEATS

ORIENTAL GLAZED TENDERLOINS

⅓ cup KIKKOMAN® Teriyaki Baste & Glaze
1 tablespoon dry sherry
½ teaspoon ginger juice*
¼ teaspoon grated orange peel
2 pork tenderloins (¾ pound each)

*Press enough fresh ginger root pieces through garlic press to measure ½ teaspoon juice.

Combine teriyaki baste & glaze, sherry, ginger juice and orange peel; set aside. Place tenderloins on grill 4 to 5 inches from hot coals. Cook 25 minutes, turning over occasionally. Brush both sides of tenderloins with baste & glaze mixture. Cook 10 minutes longer, or until meat thermometer inserted into thickest part of meat registers 160°F, turning over and brushing frequently with remaining baste & glaze mixture. Let stand 10 minutes. To serve, cut meat across grain into thin slices. *Makes 4 to 6 servings*

PEPPERY T–BONE STEAKS AND CHILI CORN

4 ears fresh sweet corn, unhusked
Cold water
1 to 2 cloves garlic, crushed
½ teaspoon black pepper
2 beef T-bone steaks, cut 1 to 1½ inches thick
2 tablespoons butter or margarine
½ teaspoon chili powder
¼ teaspoon ground cumin

Pull back corn husks from each ear of corn, leaving husks attached to base. Remove corn silk. Fold husks back around corn; tie at end of each ear with string. Soak corn in cold water 3 to 4 hours.

Prepare grill. Remove corn from water. Place on grid. Grill over medium coals 20 minutes, turning often. Meanwhile, combine garlic and pepper; rub evenly into both sides of steaks. Place steaks on grid with corn; grill steaks to desired doneness, turning steaks once and corn often. (Grill 1-inch-thick steaks 10 to 14 minutes for rare to medium. Grill 1½-inch-thick steaks 22 to 30 minutes for rare to medium.) Remove corn when tender. Meanwhile, melt butter. Stir in chili powder and cumin; keep warm. Trim excess fat before carving steaks into thick slices. Serve with corn and seasoned butter. *Makes 4 servings*

*Favorite recipe from **National Cattlemen's Beef Association***

STICK-TO-THE-RIBS MEATS

SOUTHWESTERN LAMB CHOPS WITH CHARRED CORN RELISH

**4 lamb shoulder or blade chops
(about 2 pounds), cut ¾ inch thick,
well trimmed**
¼ cup vegetable oil
¼ cup fresh lime juice
1 tablespoon chili powder
2 cloves garlic, minced
1 teaspoon ground cumin
¼ teaspoon ground red pepper
Charred Corn Relish (recipe follows)
2 tablespoons chopped cilantro
Hot pepper jelly (optional)

1. Place chops in large resealable plastic food storage bag. Combine oil, lime juice, chili powder, garlic, cumin and ground red pepper in small bowl; mix well. Reserve 3 tablespoons mixture for Charred Corn Relish; cover and refrigerate. Pour remaining mixture over chops. Seal bag tightly, turning to coat. Marinate in refrigerator at least 8 hours or overnight, turning occasionally.

2. Prepare barbecue grill for direct cooking.

3. Meanwhile, prepare Charred Corn Relish.

4. Drain chops; discard marinade from bag. Place chops on grid. Grill chops, on covered grill, over medium coals 13 to 15 minutes for medium or until desired doneness is reached, turning halfway through grilling time. Sprinkle with cilantro. Serve with Charred Corn Relish and hot pepper jelly.

Makes 4 servings

Charred Corn Relish

2 large or 3 small ears fresh corn, shucked
½ cup diced red bell pepper
¼ cup chopped cilantro
3 tablespoons reserved lime mixture

1. Place corn on grid. Grill corn, on covered grill, over medium coals 10 to 12 minutes or until charred, turning occasionally. Cool to room temperature.

2. Holding tip of 1 ear, stand upright on its stem end in medium bowl. Cut down the sides of cob with paring knife, releasing kernels without cutting into cob.

3. Press down along each cob with dull edge of utility knife to release any remaining corn and liquid.

4. Add bell pepper, cilantro and reserved lime mixture to corn; mix well. Let stand at room temperature while grilling chops. Cover; refrigerate if preparing in advance. Bring to room temperature before serving.

Makes about 1½ cups

Southwestern Lamb Chop with Charred Corn Relish

GRILLED MEAT LOAF

1½ **pounds ground chuck or ground sirloin**
½ **cup seasoned dry bread crumbs**
⅓ **cup shredded onion**
⅔ **cup chili sauce, divided**
1 **egg**
½ **teaspoon pepper**
¼ **teaspoon salt**
2 **tablespoons packed light brown sugar**
1 **tablespoon spicy brown or Dijon-style mustard**

1. Prepare grill. Combine beef, bread crumbs, onion, ⅓ cup chili sauce, egg, pepper and salt in large bowl; mix well. On cutting board or cookie sheet, shape mixture into oval loaf 1½ inches thick, about 9 inches long and 5 inches wide.

2. Combine remaining ⅓ cup chili sauce, sugar and mustard in small bowl; mix well. Set aside. Place meat loaf on grid. Grill meat loaf, on covered grill, over medium-hot coals 10 minutes. Carefully turn meat loaf over using 2 large spatulas.

3. Brush chili sauce mixture over top of meat loaf. Continue to grill, covered, 10 to 12 minutes for medium-well or until desired doneness is reached. (If desired, insert instant-read thermometer* into center of thickest part of meat loaf. Thermometer should register 160°F for medium-well.) Let stand 10 minutes before slicing. Serve with mashed potatoes and peas and carrots, if desired.

Makes 4 to 6 servings

*Do not leave instant-read thermometer in meat loaf during grilling since the thermometer is not heatproof.

CHARCOAL BEEF KABOBS

½ **cup vegetable oil**
¼ **cup lemon juice**
1½ **tablespoons (½ package) HIDDEN VALLEY RANCH® Salad Dressing Mix**
2 **pounds beef top round or boneless sirloin steak, cut into 1-inch cubes**
1 *or* 2 **red, yellow or green bell peppers, cut into 1-inch squares**
16 **pearl onions** *or* 1 **medium onion, cut into wedges**
8 **cherry tomatoes**

Combine oil, lemon juice and dry salad dressing mix. Pour over beef cubes in shallow dish. Cover and refrigerate 1 hour or longer. Drain beef; reserve marinade. Thread beef cubes, peppers and onions onto skewers. Grill kabobs, on uncovered grill, over medium-hot KINGSFORD® Briquets 15 minutes, brushing often with reserved marinade and turning to brown all sides. A few minutes before serving, add cherry tomatoes to ends of skewers. (Do not baste during last 5 minutes of grilling.)

Grilled Meat Loaf

STICK-TO-THE-RIBS MEATS

GRILLED PORK AND POTATOES VESUVIO

> **1 center-cut boneless pork loin roast (1½ pounds), well trimmed and cut into 1-inch cubes**
> **½ cup dry white wine**
> **2 tablespoons olive oil**
> **4 cloves garlic, minced, divided**
> **1½ to 2 pounds small red potatoes (about 1½ inches in diameter), scrubbed**
> **6 metal skewers (12 inches long)**
> **6 lemon wedges**
> **Salt (optional)**
> **Pepper (optional)**
> **¼ cup chopped fresh Italian or curly leaf parsley**
> **1 teaspoon finely grated lemon peel**

1. Place pork in large resealable plastic food storage bag. Combine wine, oil and 3 cloves garlic in small bowl; pour over pork.

2. Place potatoes in single layer in microwave-safe dish. Pierce each potato with tip of sharp knife. Microwave at HIGH (100% power) 6 to 7 minutes or until almost tender when pierced with fork. (Or, place potatoes in large saucepan. Cover with cold water. Bring to a boil over high heat. Simmer about 12 minutes or until almost tender when pierced with fork.) Immediately rinse with cold water; drain.

3. Add to pork in bag. Seal bag tightly, turning to coat. Marinate in refrigerator at least 2 hours or up to 8 hours, turning occasionally.

4. Prepare barbecue grill for direct cooking.

5. Meanwhile, drain pork mixture; discard marinade. Alternately thread about 3 pork cubes and 2 potatoes onto each skewer. Place 1 lemon wedge on end of each skewer. Sprinkle salt and pepper over pork and potatoes.

6. Place skewers on grid. Grill skewers, on covered grill, over medium coals 14 to 16 minutes or until pork is juicy and barely pink in center and potatoes are tender, turning halfway through grilling time.

7. Remove skewers from grill. Combine parsley, lemon peel and remaining minced garlic clove in small bowl. Sprinkle over pork and potatoes. Squeeze lemon wedges over pork and potatoes.

Makes 6 servings

STICK-TO-THE-RIBS MEATS

ROSEMARY–CRUSTED LEG OF LAMB

¼ cup Dijon-style mustard
2 large cloves garlic, minced
1 boneless butterflied leg of lamb (sirloin half, about 2½ pounds), well trimmed
3 tablespoons chopped fresh rosemary leaves *or* 1 tablespoon dried rosemary leaves, crushed
Fresh rosemary sprigs (optional)
Mint jelly (optional)

Prepare grill. Combine mustard and garlic in small bowl; spread half of mixture with fingers or spatula over one side of lamb. Sprinkle with half of chopped rosemary; pat into mustard mixture. Turn lamb over; repeat with remaining mustard mixture and rosemary. Insert meat thermometer into center of thickest part of lamb.

Place lamb on grid. Grill lamb, on covered grill, over medium coals 35 to 40 minutes or until thermometer registers 160°F for medium or until desired doneness is reached, turning every 10 minutes.

Soak rosemary sprigs in water. Place rosemary sprigs directly on coals during last 10 minutes of grilling. Transfer lamb to carving board; tent with foil. Let stand 10 minutes before carving into thin slices. Serve with mint jelly.   *Makes 8 servings*

RANCH–STYLE FAJITAS

2 pounds flank or skirt steak
½ cup vegetable oil
⅓ cup lime juice
2 packages (1 ounce each) HIDDEN VALLEY RANCH® Milk Recipe Original Ranch® Salad Dressing Mix
1 teaspoon ground cumin
½ teaspoon black pepper
6 flour tortillas
Lettuce
Guacamole, prepared Hidden Valley Ranch® Salad Dressing and picante sauce, for toppings

Place steak in large baking dish. In small bowl, whisk together oil, lime juice, salad dressing mix, cumin and pepper. Pour mixture over steak. Cover and refrigerate several hours or overnight.

Remove steak; reserve marinade. Grill steak over medium-hot coals to desired doneness, basting with reserved marinade. (Or, broil steak to desired doneness.) Remove steak and slice diagonally across grain into thin slices. Heat tortillas to soften, following package directions. Divide steak strips among tortillas; roll to enclose. Serve with lettuce and desired toppings.   *Makes 6 servings*

STICK-TO-THE-RIBS MEATS

PEPPERED BEEF RIB ROAST

1½ tablespoons black peppercorns
1 boneless beef rib roast (2½ to 3 pounds), well trimmed
¼ cup Dijon mustard
2 cloves garlic, minced
¾ cup sour cream
2 tablespoons prepared horseradish
1 tablespoon balsamic vinegar
½ teaspoon sugar

Prepare grill with rectangular metal or foil drip pan. Bank briquets on either side of drip pan for indirect cooking. Meanwhile, place peppercorns in heavy, small resealable plastic food storage bag. Squeeze out excess air; seal bag tightly. Pound peppercorns using flat side of meat mallet or rolling pin until cracked. Pat roast dry with paper towels. Combine mustard and garlic in small bowl; spread with spatula over top and sides of roast. Sprinkle cracked pepper over mustard mixture.

Insert meat thermometer into center of thickest part of roast. Place roast, pepper side up, on grid directly over drip pan. Grill, on covered grill, over medium coals 60 to 70 minutes or until thermometer registers 150°F for medium-rare or to desired doneness, adding 4 to 9 briquets to both sides of fire after 45 minutes to maintain medium coals. Meanwhile, combine sour cream, horseradish, vinegar and sugar in small bowl; mix well. Cover; refrigerate until serving. Transfer roast to carving board; tent with foil. Let stand 5 to 10 minutes before carving. Serve with horseradish sauce mixture.   *Makes 6 to 8 servings*

CURRIED PORK KABOBS

1 pound boneless pork loin, cut into ½-inch cubes
1 cup low-fat plain yogurt
2 tablespoons orange juice
1 tablespoon ground coriander
½ teaspoon ground turmeric
½ teaspoon ground cumin
½ teaspoon salt
¼ teaspoon ground ginger

For marinade, combine all ingredients except pork cubes in medium bowl; blend well. Add pork; stir to coat with marinade. Cover and refrigerate 4 hours or overnight.

Prepare grill. Remove pork; discard marinade. Lightly pat pork dry with paper towels. Thread pork evenly onto skewers.* Grill over medium-hot coals about 10 minutes or until pork is nicely browned and barely pink in center, turning frequently. Serve immediately.   *Makes 4 servings*

*If using bamboo skewers, soak in cold water 30 minutes to prevent burning.

Favorite recipe from **National Pork Producers Council**

Curried Pork Kabob

STICK-TO-THE-RIBS MEATS

MINT MARINATED RACKS OF LAMB

- 2 whole racks (6 ribs each) loin lamb chops (about 3 pounds), well trimmed
- 1 cup dry red wine
- ½ cup chopped fresh mint leaves (optional)
- 3 cloves garlic, minced
- ¼ cup Dijon mustard
- 2 tablespoons chopped fresh mint leaves *or* 2 teaspoons dried mint leaves, crushed
- ⅔ cup dry bread crumbs

Place lamb in large resealable plastic food storage bag. Combine wine, ½ cup mint and garlic in small bowl. Pour over chops. Seal bag tightly; turn to coat. Marinate in refrigerator at least 2 hours or up to 4 hours, turning occasionally.

Prepare grill. Drain lamb, discarding marinade. Pat lamb dry with paper towels. Place lamb in shallow glass dish or on cutting board. Combine mustard and 2 tablespoons mint in small bowl; spread over meaty side of lamb. Pat bread crumbs evenly over mustard mixture. Place lamb, crumb side down, on grid. Grill, on covered grill, over medium coals 10 minutes. Carefully turn; continue to grill, covered, 20 to 22 minutes more for medium or to desired doneness. Place lamb on carving board. Slice between ribs into individual chops.

Makes 4 servings

HONEY–LIME PORK CHOPS

- 1 envelope LIPTON® Recipe Secrets® Savory Herb with Garlic or Onion Soup Mix
- 3 tablespoons soy sauce
- 2 tablespoons honey
- 2 tablespoons lime juice
- 1 teaspoon grated fresh ginger *or* ¼ teaspoon ground ginger (optional)
- 4 boneless pork chops, 1½ inches thick (about 1 pound)

In 13×9-inch glass baking dish, blend all ingredients except pork chops; add chops and turn to coat. Cover and marinate in refrigerator, turning chops occasionally, at least 2 hours. Remove chops, reserving marinade.

Grill or broil chops 15 to 18 minutes or until pork is juicy and barely pink in center, turning once and basting with reserved marinade. (Do not baste during last 5 minutes of grilling.)

Makes about 4 servings

Mint Marinated Racks of Lamb

STICK-TO-THE-RIBS MEATS

SEASONED BABY BACK RIBS

1 tablespoon paprika
1½ teaspoons garlic salt
1 teaspoon celery salt
½ teaspoon black pepper
¼ teaspoon ground red pepper
4 pounds pork baby back ribs, cut into
    3- to 4-rib portions, well trimmed
Barbecue Sauce (recipe follows)
Orange peel for garnish

Preheat oven to 350°F. Combine paprika, garlic salt, celery salt, black pepper and ground red pepper in small bowl. Rub over all surfaces of ribs. Place ribs in foil-lined shallow roasting pan. Bake 30 minutes. Meanwhile, prepare grill. While coals are heating, prepare Barbecue Sauce.

Place ribs directly on grid. Grill ribs, on covered grill, over medium coals 10 minutes. Remove ribs with tongs; brush with half the Barbecue Sauce over both sides. Return ribs to grill. Continue to grill, covered, 10 minutes or until ribs are tender and browned. Serve with reserved sauce. Garnish, if desired. *Makes 6 servings*

Barbecue Sauce
½ cup ketchup
⅓ cup packed light brown sugar
1 tablespoon cider vinegar
2 teaspoons Worcestershire sauce
2 teaspoons soy sauce

Combine all ingredients in small bowl. Reserve half of sauce for serving. *Makes about ⅔ cup*

BARBECUED PORK LOIN

2 teaspoons LAWRY'S® Seasoned Salt
1 (3- to 3½-pound) boneless pork loin
1 cup orange juice
¼ cup soy sauce
1 teaspoon LAWRY'S® Garlic Powder with
    Parsley
½ teaspoon LAWRY'S® Seasoned Pepper
Vegetable oil

Sprinkle Seasoned Salt onto all sides of meat. In large resealable plastic bag or shallow glass baking dish, place meat; let stand 10 to 15 minutes. Combine orange juice, soy sauce, Garlic Powder with Parsley and Seasoned Pepper; pour over meat. Seal bag or cover dish. Marinate in refrigerator at least 2 hours or overnight, turning occasionally. Heat grill for medium coals; brush grid with vegetable oil. Remove meat, reserving marinade. Grill, 4 to 5 inches from heat, 30 minutes or until internal meat temperature reaches 170°F, turning and brushing frequently with reserved marinade. Remove meat from grill; let stand about 10 minutes before thinly slicing. Meanwhile, in small saucepan, bring remaining marinade to a boil; boil 1 minute. *Makes 6 servings*

Seasoned Baby Back Ribs

— *Abounding* —

POULTRY PICKS

MAPLE–GLAZED TURKEY BREAST

1 bone-in turkey breast (5 to 6 pounds)
¼ cup pure maple syrup
2 tablespoons butter or margarine, melted
1 tablespoon bourbon (optional)
2 teaspoons freshly grated orange peel
Fresh bay leaves for garnish

Prepare grill with rectangular metal or foil drip pan. Bank briquets on either side of drip pan for indirect cooking. Insert meat thermometer into thickest part of turkey, not touching bone. Place bone side down, on grid. Grill, on covered grill, over medium coals 55 minutes, adding 4 to 9 briquets to both sides of fire after 45 minutes to maintain medium coals.

Combine syrup, butter, bourbon and orange peel in small bowl; brush half of mixture over turkey. Grill, covered, 10 minutes. Brush with remaining mixture; grill, covered, about 10 minutes or until thermometer registers 170°F. Transfer turkey to carving board; tent with foil. Let stand 10 minutes before carving. Cut turkey into thin slices. Garnish, if desired. *Makes 6 to 8 servings*

POULTRY PICKS

GRILLED CHICKEN TOSTADAS

- **1 pound boneless skinless chicken breast halves**
- **1 teaspoon ground cumin**
- **¼ cup fresh orange juice**
- **¼ cup plus 2 tablespoons hot or mild salsa, divided**
- **1 tablespoon vegetable oil**
- **2 cloves garlic, minced**
- **8 green onions**
  Additional vegetable oil
- **1 can (16 ounces) refried beans**
- **4 (10-inch) *or* 8 (6- to 7-inch) flour tortillas**
- **2 cups sliced romaine lettuce leaves**
- **1½ cups (6 ounces) shredded Monterey Jack cheese with jalapeño peppers**
- **1 ripe medium avocado, pitted and diced (optional)**
- **1 medium tomato, seeded and coarsely chopped**
  Chopped cilantro (optional)
  Sour cream

1. Place chicken in single layer in shallow glass dish; sprinkle with cumin. Combine orange juice, ¼ cup salsa, 1 tablespoon oil and garlic in small bowl; pour over chicken. Cover; marinate in refrigerator at least 2 hours or up to 8 hours, stirring mixture occasionally.

2. Prepare grill. Drain chicken; reserve marinade. Brush green onions with additional oil. Place chicken and green onions on grid. Grill, on covered grill, over medium-hot coals 5 minutes. Brush tops of chicken with half of reserved marinade; turn and brush with remaining marinade. Turn onions. Continue to grill, covered, 5 minutes or until chicken is no longer pink in center and onions are tender. (If onions are browning too quickly, remove before chicken is done.)

3. Meanwhile, combine beans and remaining 2 tablespoons salsa in small saucepan; cook, stirring occasionally, over medium heat until hot.

4. Place tortillas in single layer on grid. Grill tortillas, on uncovered grill, 1 to 2 minutes per side or until golden brown. (If tortillas puff up, pierce with tip of knife or flatten by pressing with spatula.)

5. Transfer chicken and onions to carving board. Slice chicken crosswise into ½-inch-wide strips. Cut green onions crosswise into 1-inch-long pieces. Spread tortillas with bean mixture; top with lettuce, chicken, onions, cheese, avocado and tomato. Sprinkle with cilantro. Serve with sour cream.
Makes 4 servings

Grilled Chicken Tostada

POULTRY PICKS

MESQUITE–GRILLED TURKEY

2 cups mesquite chips, divided
1 fresh or thawed frozen turkey
**   (10 to 12 pounds)**
1 small sweet or Spanish onion, peeled and
**   quartered**
1 lemon, quartered
3 fresh tarragon sprigs
1 metal skewer (6 inches long)
2 tablespoons butter or margarine, softened
**   Salt and pepper (optional)**
**   Additional fresh tarragon sprigs (optional)**
¼ cup butter or margarine, melted
2 tablespoons fresh lemon juice
2 tablespoons chopped fresh tarragon
**   leaves *or* 2 teaspoons dried tarragon**
**   leaves, crushed**
2 cloves garlic, minced

1. Prepare grill with rectangular metal or foil drip pan. Bank briquets on either side of drip pan for indirect cooking. Cover mesquite chips with cold water; soak 20 minutes.

2. Remove giblets from turkey cavity; reserve for another use. Rinse turkey with cold running water; pat dry with paper towels. Place onion, lemon and 3 tarragon sprigs in cavity. Pull skin over neck; secure with metal skewer. Tuck wing tips under back; tie legs together with wet kitchen string.

3. Using fingers or paper towel, spread softened butter over turkey skin; sprinkle with salt and pepper to taste. Insert meat thermometer into center of thickest part of thigh, not touching bone.

4. Drain mesquite chips; sprinkle 1 cup over coals. Place turkey, breast side up, on grid directly over drip pan. Grill turkey, on covered grill, over medium coals 11 to 14 minutes per pound, adding 4 to 9 briquets to both sides of fire each hour to maintain medium coals and adding remaining 1 cup mesquite chips after 1 hour of grilling. Meanwhile, soak additional fresh tarragon sprigs in water.

5. Combine melted butter, lemon juice, chopped tarragon and garlic in small bowl. Brush half of mixture over turkey during last 30 minutes of grilling. Place soaked tarragon sprigs directly on coals. Continue to grill, covered, 20 minutes. Brush with remaining mixture. Continue to grill, covered, about 10 minutes or until thermometer registers 180°F.

6. Transfer turkey to carving board; tent with foil. Let stand 15 minutes before carving. Discard onion, lemon and tarragon sprigs from cavity.

Makes 8 to 10 servings

Mesquite-Grilled Turkey

POULTRY PICKS

LEMON–GARLIC ROASTED CHICKEN

1 chicken (3½ to 4 pounds)
Salt and black pepper
2 tablespoons butter or margarine, softened
2 lemons, cut into halves
4 to 6 cloves garlic, peeled and left whole
5 to 6 sprigs fresh rosemary
Garlic Sauce (recipe follows)
Additional rosemary sprigs and lemon
wedges

Rinse chicken; pat dry with paper towels. Season with salt and pepper, then rub the skin with butter. Place lemons, garlic and rosemary in cavity of chicken. Tuck wings under back and tie legs together with cotton string.

Arrange medium-low KINGSFORD® Briquets on each side of rectangular metal or foil drip pan. Pour in hot tap water to fill pan half full. Place chicken, breast side up, on grid directly above drip pan. Grill chicken, on covered grill, about 1 hour or until meat thermometer inserted in thigh registers 175° to 180°F or until joints move easily and juices run clear when chicken is pierced. Add a few briquets to both sides of fire, if necessary, to maintain constant temperature.

While chicken is cooking, prepare Garlic Sauce. When chicken is done, carefully lift it from grill to wide shallow bowl so that all juices from cavity run into bowl. Transfer juices to small bowl or gravy boat. Carve chicken; serve with Garlic Sauce and cooking juices. Garnish with rosemary sprigs and lemon wedges. *Makes 4 servings*

Garlic Sauce

2 tablespoons olive oil
1 large head of garlic, cloves separated and
peeled
2 (1-inch-wide) strips lemon peel
1 can (14½ ounces) low-salt chicken broth
½ cup water
1 sprig each sage and oregano *or* 2 to
3 sprigs parsley
¼ cup butter, softened

Heat oil in saucepan; add garlic cloves and lemon peel. Cook and stir over medium-low heat, stirring frequently, until garlic just starts to brown in a few spots. Add broth, water and herbs; simmer to reduce mixture by about half. Discard herb sprigs and lemon peel. Transfer broth mixture to blender or food processor; process until smooth. Return garlic purée to saucepan and whisk in butter over very low heat until smooth. Sauce can be rewarmed before serving. *Makes about 1 cup*

TIP: The chicken is delicious served simply with its own juices, but the Garlic Sauce is so good you may want to double the recipe.

Lemon-Garlic Roasted Chicken

POULTRY PICKS

MARINATED TURKEY & VEGETABLE KABOBS

½ cup **MIRACLE WHIP® FREE® Dressing**
½ cup **KRAFT® FREE® Italian Nonfat Dressing**
¼ teaspoon **garlic powder**
⅛ teaspoon **ground red pepper**
1 pound **fresh boneless skinless turkey breast, cut into 1-inch cubes**
2 cups **cherry tomatoes**
2 **zucchini, cut into ½-inch slices**
1 **yellow bell pepper, cut into 1-inch chunks**

• Mix together dressings and seasonings until well blended; reserve ¼ cup dressing mixture. Pour remaining dressing mixture over turkey. Cover; marinate in refrigerator at least 20 minutes. Drain marinade; discard.

• Arrange turkey and vegetables on skewers. Place on grill over hot coals (coals will be glowing). Grill, uncovered, 10 minutes on each side or until tender, brushing frequently with reserved ¼ cup dressing mixture. *Makes 4 servings*

CHICKEN RIBBONS SATAY

½ cup **creamy peanut butter**
½ cup **water**
¼ cup **soy sauce**
4 **cloves garlic, pressed**
3 tablespoons **lemon juice**
2 tablespoons **firmly packed brown sugar**
¾ teaspoon **ground ginger**
½ teaspoon **crushed red pepper flakes**
4 **boneless skinless chicken breast halves**
Sliced green onion tops for garnish

Combine peanut butter, water, soy sauce, garlic, lemon juice, brown sugar, ginger and red pepper flakes in small saucepan. Cook over medium heat 1 minute or until smooth; cool. Remove garlic from sauce; discard. Reserve half of sauce for dipping. Cut chicken lengthwise into 1-inch-wide strips. Thread onto 8 metal or bamboo skewers. (Soak bamboo skewers in water at least 20 minutes to keep them from burning.)

Oil hot grid to help prevent sticking. Grill chicken, on covered grill, over medium-hot KINGSFORD® Briquets, 6 to 8 minutes until chicken is cooked through, turning once. Baste with sauce once or twice during cooking. Serve with reserved sauce garnished with sliced green onion tops. *Makes 4 servings*

Chicken Ribbons Satay

POULTRY PICKS

BUFFALO CHICKEN DRUMSTICKS

8 large chicken drumsticks
  (about 2 pounds)
3 tablespoons hot pepper sauce
1 tablespoon vegetable oil
1 clove garlic, minced
¼ cup mayonnaise
3 tablespoons sour cream
1½ tablespoons white wine vinegar
¼ teaspoon sugar
⅓ cup (1½ ounces) crumbled Roquefort or
  blue cheese
2 cups hickory chips
  Celery sticks

1. Place chicken in large resealable plastic food storage bag. Combine hot pepper sauce, oil and garlic in small bowl; pour over chicken. Seal bag tightly, turning to coat. Marinate in refrigerator at least 1 hour or, for hotter flavor, up to 24 hours, turning occasionally.

2. Combine mayonnaise, sour cream, vinegar and sugar in another small bowl. Stir in cheese; cover and refrigerate until serving.

3. Prepare grill. Cover hickory chips with cold water; soak 20 minutes. Drain chicken; discard marinade. Drain hickory chips; sprinkle over coals. Place chicken on grid. Grill chicken, on covered grill, over medium-hot coals 25 to 30 minutes or until chicken is no longer pink in center and juices run clear, turning 3 to 4 times. Serve with blue cheese dressing and celery sticks.

Makes 4 servings

CHILI ROASTED TURKEY BREAST

1 envelope LIPTON® Recipe Secrets® Onion
  Soup Mix*
¼ cup vegetable oil
1½ teaspoons chili powder
1½ teaspoons fresh lime juice
½ teaspoon garlic powder (optional)
½ teaspoon ground cumin
¼ teaspoon dried oregano leaves
1 (5-pound) turkey breast (with bone)

*Also terrific with Lipton® Recipe Secrets® Onion-Mushroom or Beefy Onion Soup Mix.

Preheat oven to 350°F. In small bowl, blend all ingredients except turkey; let stand 5 minutes. In large roasting pan, place turkey, breast side up. Brush soup mixture onto turkey; tent with foil. Roast 1 hour, basting once. Remove foil and continue roasting 1 hour or until meat thermometer reaches 180°F. Let stand, tented with aluminum foil, 10 minutes.

Makes about 6 servings

Buffalo Chicken Drumsticks

POULTRY PICKS

GRILLED TURKEY WITH WALNUT PESTO

**1 (4- to 5½-pound) turkey breast
Walnut Pesto Sauce (recipe follows)**

• Prepare coals for grilling.

• Place aluminum drip pan in center of charcoal grate under grilling rack. Arrange hot coals around drip pan.

• Place turkey on greased grill. Grill, covered, 1½ to 2 hours or until internal temperature reaches 170°F.

• Slice turkey; serve with Walnut Pesto Sauce. Garnish with red and yellow pear-shaped cherry tomatoes, fresh chives and basil leaves, if desired.

Makes 12 servings

Prep Time: 15 minutes
Cook Time: 2 hours

Walnut Pesto Sauce

**1 (8-ounce) container Light PHILADELPHIA BRAND® Pasteurized Process Cream Cheese Product
1 (7-ounce) container refrigerated prepared pesto
½ cup finely chopped walnuts, toasted
⅓ cup milk
1 garlic clove, minced
⅛ teaspoon ground red pepper**

• Stir together all ingredients in small bowl until well blended. Serve chilled or at room temperature.

BRANDY–ORANGE BARBECUED HENS

**2 PERDUE® Fresh Cornish Hens
   (1½ pounds each)
1 tablespoon vegetable oil
2 tablespoons lemon juice, divided
½ teaspoon ground ginger, divided
   Salt and pepper
¼ cup orange marmalade
1 tablespoon brandy**

Prepare coals for grilling. Rinse hens and pat dry. With kitchen string, tie drumsticks together. Rub outside of hens with oil and 1 tablespoon lemon juice; sprinkle with ¼ teaspoon ginger. Season with salt and pepper.

Combine marmalade, brandy, remaining 1 tablespoon lemon juice and remaining ¼ teaspoon ginger in small bowl; set aside. Place hens, breast side up, on grill. Grill, covered, 5 to 6 inches over medium-hot coals 50 to 60 minutes. Brush outside of hens with brandy-orange sauce after 40 minutes of grilling. Cook until juices run clear when thigh is pierced, basting additional 3 to 4 times.

Makes 2 to 4 servings

POULTRY PICKS

BBQ TURKEY WITH PINEAPPLE RELISH

2 pounds boneless, skinless turkey breast roast

MARINADE
**Grated peel and juice from 1 DOLE®
    Orange**
2 tablespoons red wine vinegar
**1½ tablespoons dried oregano leaves,
    crushed**
1 tablespoon brown sugar, packed
2 teaspoons vegetable oil
5 cloves garlic, pressed
Salt and pepper to taste

PINEAPPLE RELISH
1 DOLE® Fresh Pineapple
1 medium tomato, seeded and chopped
1 small red onion, minced
½ cup DOLE® Pitted Prunes, snipped
¼ cup chopped cilantro
2 tablespoons lime juice
1 tablespoon white vinegar
1 tablespoon drained capers

• Cut 4 (1-inch) slashes in both sides of turkey. Place in glass casserole dish.

• Combine marinade ingredients in small bowl. Pour over turkey. Cover; marinate in refrigerator 30 minutes or overnight, turning occasionally.

• Twist crown from pineapple. Cut pineapple in half lengthwise. Cut fruit from shells with knife.

Trim off core. Cut half of fruit crosswise into thin slices for garnish; reserve. Coarsely chop remaining fruit; combine with remaining relish ingredients in medium bowl.

• Drain turkey; heat marinade thoroughly. Place turkey 6 inches above medium-hot coals. Grill, uncovered, turning and basting every 5 minutes with marinade 30 to 35 minutes or until meat thermometer registers 170°F. Let stand 5 minutes. Slice; serve with Pineapple Relish. Garnish with reserved pineapple slices.   *Makes 6 servings*

GRILLED LEMON CHICKEN DIJON

**⅓ cup HOLLAND HOUSE® White with Lemon
    Cooking Wine**
⅓ cup olive oil
2 tablespoons Dijon mustard
1 teaspoon dried thyme leaves
**2 whole chicken breasts, skinned, boned
    and halved**

Combine all ingredients except chicken in shallow glass baking dish or large resealable plastic food storage bag. Add chicken and turn to coat. Cover or seal bag; marinate in refrigerator 1 to 2 hours.

Prepare grill. Drain chicken, reserving marinade. Grill chicken over medium coals 15 to 20 minutes or until no longer pink in center, turning once and basting with marinade. (Do not baste during last 5 minutes of grilling.)   *Makes 4 servings*

POULTRY PICKS

LIME SALSA CHICKEN

4 broiler-fryer chicken breast halves, boned and skinned
¼ cup lime juice
2 tablespoons sherry
2 tablespoons light olive oil
½ teaspoon dried oregano leaves
½ teaspoon garlic salt
    Salsa (recipe follows)
    Avocado slices
    Tortilla chips

For marinade, combine lime juice, sherry, oil, oregano and garlic salt in large glass bowl or resealable plastic food storage bag. Remove 3 tablespoons marinade; set aside for Salsa. Add chicken to remaining marinade; turn to coat. Cover and marinate in refrigerator 1 hour.

Meanwhile, prepare grill and Salsa. Remove chicken, reserving marinade in small saucepan. Bring marinade to a boil; cook 1 minute. Place chicken on grid. Brush marinade over chicken. Grill 8 inches over medium coals about 16 to 20 minutes or until chicken is no longer pink in center, turning and basting frequently with marinade. (Do not baste during last 5 minutes of grilling.) Arrange chicken on platter. Serve with Salsa. Garnish with avocado slices and tortilla chips. *Makes 4 servings*

SALSA: Stir together 1 peeled, seeded and chopped tomato, 1 sliced green onion, ¼ cup sliced ripe olives, 3 tablespoons reserved marinade,

1 tablespoon seeded and chopped jalapeño pepper, 1 tablespoon chopped fresh cilantro, 1 tablespoon chopped fresh mint, 1 tablespoon slivered almonds, ¼ teaspoon salt and ¼ teaspoon black pepper; refrigerate. *Makes 1 cup*

*Favorite recipe from **Delmarva Poultry Industry, Inc.***

"SMAKING" WINGS

16 chicken wings
½ cup olive or vegetable oil
¼ cup balsamic vinegar
¼ cup honey
2 tablespoons brown sugar
2 tablespoons cane syrup or dark corn syrup
1 tablespoon TABASCO® pepper sauce
½ teaspoon red pepper flakes
½ teaspoon dried thyme leaves
1 teaspoon soy sauce
¼ teaspoon Worcestershire sauce
¼ teaspoon ground red pepper
¼ teaspoon ground nutmeg

Cut off and discard bony wing tips. Cut remaining wings in half. Combine remaining ingredients in large bowl until well blended; add wings. Cover and marinate in refrigerator 1 hour.

Prepare grill. Place wings on grid. Grill 15 to 20 minutes over medium coals, turning frequently. *Makes 32 appetizers*

Lime Salsa Chicken

POULTRY PICKS

TURKEY BURRITOS

1 tablespoon ground cumin
1 tablespoon chili powder
1½ teaspoons salt
1½ to 2 pounds turkey tenderloin, cut into
    ½-inch cubes
    Avocado-Corn Salsa (recipe follows)
    Lime wedges
    Flour tortillas
    Sour cream (optional)
    Tomato slices for garnish

Combine cumin, chili powder and salt in cup. Place turkey cubes in shallow glass dish or large heavy plastic food storage bag; pour dry rub over turkey and thoroughly coat. Let turkey stand while preparing Avocado-Corn Salsa. Thread turkey on metal or bamboo skewers. (Soak bamboo skewers in water at least 20 minutes to prevent them from burning.)

Oil hot grid to help prevent sticking. Grill turkey, on covered grill, over medium KINGSFORD® Briquets, about 6 minutes until turkey is cooked through, turning once. Remove skewers from grill; squeeze lime wedges on skewers. Warm flour tortillas in microwave oven, or brush each tortilla very lightly with water and grill 10 to 15 seconds per side. Top with Avocado-Corn Salsa and sour cream, if desired. Garnish with tomato slices.

Makes 6 servings

Avocado-Corn Salsa

2 medium, ripe avocados, finely diced
1 cup cooked fresh or thawed frozen corn
2 medium tomatoes, seeded, finely diced
2 to 3 tablespoons lime juice
2 to 3 tablespoons chopped fresh cilantro
½ to 1 teaspoon minced hot green chili
    pepper
½ teaspoon salt

Gently stir together all ingredients in medium bowl; adjust flavors to taste. Cover and refrigerate until ready to serve. *Makes about 1½ cups*

GRILLED GAME HENS

½ cup K.C. MASTERPIECE® Barbecue Sauce
¼ cup dry sherry
3 tablespoons frozen orange juice
    concentrate, thawed
4 Cornish game hens (each about 1 to
    1½ pounds)

Combine barbecue sauce, sherry and orange juice concentrate in small saucepan. Bring to a boil. Simmer 10 minutes; cool. Rinse hens; pat dry with paper towels. Brush sauce onto hens. Oil hot grid. Grill hens, on covered grill, over medium-hot KINGSFORD® Briquets, 40 to 50 minutes or until thigh moves easily and juices run clear, turning once. Baste with sauce during last 10 minutes of grilling. Remove hens from grill; baste with sauce. *Makes 4 to 6 servings*

Turkey Burritos

POULTRY PICKS

HOT, SPICY, TANGY, STICKY CHICKEN

- 1 chicken (3½ to 4 pounds), cut up
- 1 cup cider vinegar
- 1 tablespoon Worcestershire sauce
- 1 tablespoon chili powder
- 1 teaspoon salt
- 1 teaspoon black pepper
- 1 teaspoon hot pepper sauce
- ¾ cup K.C. MASTERPIECE® Barbecue Sauce

Place chicken in shallow glass dish or large heavy plastic food storage bag. Combine vinegar, Worcestershire sauce, chili powder, salt, pepper and hot pepper sauce in small bowl; pour over chicken pieces. Cover dish or close bag. Marinate in refrigerator at least 4 hours, turning several times.

Oil hot grid to help prevent sticking. Place dark meat pieces on grill 10 minutes before white meat pieces (dark meat takes longer to cook). Grill chicken, on covered grill, over medium KINGSFORD® Briquets, 30 to 45 minutes, turning once or twice. Turn and baste with K.C. Masterpiece® Barbecue Sauce during last 10 minutes of cooking. Chicken is done when meat is no longer pink by bone. Remove chicken from grill; baste with sauce.   *Makes 4 servings*

CHILI TOMATO GRILLED CHICKEN

- 6 broiler-fryer chicken quarters
- 2 tablespoons vegetable oil
- ½ cup finely chopped onion
- 1 clove garlic, minced
- 1 chicken bouillon cube
- ½ cup hot water
- 1 bottle (8 ounces) taco sauce or 1 can (8 ounces) tomato sauce
- 1 teaspoon salt
- ¼ teaspoon dried oregano leaves
- 2 tablespoons vinegar
- 1 tablespoon prepared mustard
- 3 teaspoons mild chili powder, divided

In small skillet, place oil and heat to medium temperature. Add onion and garlic; stir and cook about 3 minutes or until clear and soft. Dissolve bouillon cube in hot water; add bouillon to skillet, along with taco sauce, salt, oregano, vinegar and mustard. Dip chicken into sauce mixture; then sprinkle 2 teaspoons chili powder on all sides of chicken. Add remaining 1 teaspoon chili powder to sauce; bring to a boil and remove from heat. Redip each quarter in sauce. Place chicken on prepared grill, skin side up, about 8 inches from heat. Grill, turning every 15 minutes, about 60 minutes or until fork tender and juices run clear. Brush generously with sauce during last 30 minutes of grilling.   *Makes 6 servings*

*Favorite recipe from **National Broiler Council***

Hot, Spicy, Tangy, Sticky Chicken

POULTRY PICKS

PESTO–STUFFED GRILLED CHICKEN

2 cloves garlic, peeled
½ cup fresh basil leaves
2 tablespoons toasted pine nuts or walnuts
¼ teaspoon pepper
5 tablespoons extra-virgin olive oil, divided
¼ cup grated Parmesan cheese
1 fresh or thawed frozen roasting chicken or capon (6 to 7 pounds)
2 tablespoons fresh lemon juice
Additional fresh basil leaves and fresh red currants for garnish

1. Prepare barbecue grill with rectangular metal or foil drip pan. Bank briquets on either side of drip pan for indirect cooking.

2. Drop garlic cloves through feed tube of food processor with motor running. Add basil, pine nuts and pepper; process until basil is minced. With processor running, add 3 tablespoons oil in slow, steady stream until smooth paste forms, scraping down side of bowl once. Add cheese; process until well blended.

3. Remove giblets from chicken cavity; reserve for another use. Rinse chicken with cold water; pat dry with paper towels. Loosen skin over breast of chicken by pushing fingers between skin and meat, taking care not to tear skin. Do not loosen skin over wings and drumsticks. Using rubber spatula or small spoon, spread pesto under breast skin; massage skin to evenly spread pesto.

4. Combine remaining 2 tablespoons oil and lemon juice in small bowl; brush over chicken skin.

5. Insert meat thermometer into center of thickest part of thigh, not touching bone. Tuck wings under back; tie legs together with wet kitchen string. Place chicken, breast side up, on grid directly over drip pan. Grill chicken, on covered grill, over medium-low coals 1 hour 10 minutes to 1 hour 30 minutes or until thermometer registers 185°F, adding 4 to 9 briquets to both sides of fire after 45 minutes to maintain medium-low coals.

6. Transfer chicken to carving board; tent with foil. Let stand 15 minutes before carving. Garnish, if desired.   *Makes 6 servings*

GRILLED ITALIAN CHICKEN

½ cup prepared HIDDEN VALLEY RANCH® Ranch Italian Salad Dressing
1 tablespoon Dijon-style mustard
4 boned chicken breast halves

In small bowl or measuring cup, whisk together salad dressing and mustard; reserve 3 tablespoons for final baste. Brush chicken generously with some of remaining dressing mixture. Grill or broil, basting several times with dressing mixture, until chicken is golden and cooked through, about 5 minutes on each side. Brush generously with reserved dressing just before removing from grill.
Makes 4 servings

Pesto-Stuffed Grilled Chicken

— *Succulent* —

SEAFOOD FAVORITES

GRILLED PRAWNS WITH SALSA VERA CRUZ

1 can (14½ ounces) DEL MONTE® Mexican
  Recipe Stewed Tomatoes
1 orange, peeled and chopped
¼ cup sliced green onions
¼ cup chopped cilantro or parsley
1 tablespoon olive oil
1 to 2 teaspoons minced jalapeño chile
1 small clove garlic, crushed
1 pound medium shrimp, peeled and
  deveined

Drain tomatoes, reserving liquid; chop tomatoes. In medium bowl, combine tomatoes, reserved liquid, orange, green onions, cilantro, oil, jalapeño and garlic. Season to taste with salt and pepper, if desired. Thread shrimp on skewers; season with salt and pepper, if desired. Brush grill with oil. Cook shrimp over hot coals about 3 minutes per side or until shrimp just turn opaque pink. Top with salsa. Serve over rice, if desired. *Makes 4 servings*

HELPFUL HINT: Thoroughly rinse shrimp in cold water before cooking.

SEAFOOD FAVORITES

MEDITERRANEAN GRILLED SNAPPER

1 whole red snapper (about 4½ pounds), scaled, gutted and cavity cut open*
2 tablespoons fresh lemon juice
Salt and pepper
3 tablespoons olive oil, divided
2 tablespoons chopped fresh oregano leaves *or* 2 teaspoons dried oregano leaves, crushed
2 tablespoons chopped fresh basil leaves *or* 2 teaspoons dried basil leaves, crushed
4 slices lemon
1 metal skewer (6 inches long)
3 whole heads garlic**
Hinged fish basket (optional)
Fresh oregano sprigs (optional)
6 slices Italian bread, cut 1 inch thick
Additional olive oil (optional)

*This can be done by your fish retailer at the time of purchase or you may wish to do this yourself.

**The whole garlic bulb is called a head.

Prepare grill. Rinse snapper under cold water; pat dry with paper towels. Open cavity of snapper; brush with lemon juice. Sprinkle with salt and pepper. Combine 1 tablespoon oil, chopped oregano and basil in small bowl. Spread mixture inside cavity of snapper. Place lemon slices in cavity; close snapper. Secure opening by threading skewer lengthwise through outside edge of cavity.

Cut off top third of garlic heads to expose cloves; discard. Place each head on small sheet of heavy-duty foil; drizzle evenly with remaining 2 tablespoons oil. Wrap in foil. Place packets directly on medium-hot coals. Place snapper in oiled, hinged fish basket or on oiled grid. Grill snapper and garlic, on uncovered grill, over medium-hot coals 20 to 25 minutes or until snapper flakes easily when tested with fork, turning halfway through grilling time.

Soak oregano sprigs in water. Place sprigs directly on coals during last 10 minutes of grilling. Brush bread lightly with additional oil. During last 5 minutes of grilling, place bread around outer edges of grid to toast, about 4 minutes, turning once.

Transfer snapper to carving board. Carefully unwrap garlic. Peel off charred papery outer skin. Using pot holder, squeeze softened garlic from heads into small bowl; mash to a paste with wooden spoon or potato masher, adding additional oil. Spread bread with garlic paste. Remove skewer from snapper. Slit skin from head to tail along back and belly of snapper; pull skin from top side of snapper with fingers. Discard skin. Using knife, separate top fillet from backbone; cut into serving-size pieces. Lift up tail; pull forward to free backbone from lower fillet. Cut lower fillet into serving-size pieces. Remove skin, if desired.

Makes 6 servings

NOTE: A whole red snapper may not fit in hinged fish basket. If desired, remove head and tail.

Mediterranean Grilled Snapper

SEAFOOD FAVORITES

BLACKENED SEA BASS

    Hardwood charcoal*
2 teaspoons paprika
1 teaspoon garlic salt
1 teaspoon dried thyme leaves, crushed
¼ teaspoon ground white pepper
¼ teaspoon ground red pepper
¼ teaspoon ground black pepper
3 tablespoons butter or margarine
4 skinless sea bass or catfish fillets
    (4 to 6 ounces each)
    Lemon halves
    Fresh dill sprigs for garnish

*Hardwood charcoal takes somewhat longer than regular charcoal to become hot, but results in a hotter fire than regular charcoal. A hot fire is necessary to seal in juices and cook fish quickly. If hardwood charcoal is not available, scatter dry hardwood, mesquite or hickory chunks over hot coals to create a hot fire.

1. Prepare grill. Meanwhile, combine paprika, garlic salt, thyme and white, red and black peppers in small bowl; mix well. Set aside. Melt butter in small saucepan over medium heat. Pour melted butter into pie plate or shallow bowl. Cool slightly.

2. Dip sea bass into melted butter, evenly coating both sides. Sprinkle both sides of sea bass evenly with paprika mixture.

3. Place sea bass on grid. (Fire will flare up when sea bass is placed on grid, but will subside when grill is covered.) Grill sea bass, on covered grill, over hot coals 4 to 6 minutes or until sea bass is blackened and flakes easily when tested with fork, turning halfway through grilling time. Serve with lemon halves. Garnish, if desired.

Makes 4 servings

SCALLOP KABOBS

1 pound large sea scallops
1 green bell pepper, seeded and cut into
    1-inch chunks
1 cup small mushrooms, wiped clean
1 cup cubed fresh pineapple
¼ cup FRENCH'S® Bold'n Spicy® Mustard
¼ cup FRENCH'S® Worcestershire Sauce
¼ cup (½ stick) butter or margarine, melted

Thread scallops, pepper, mushrooms and pineapple alternately onto metal skewers. Combine remaining ingredients; brush onto skewers.

Place skewers on oiled grid. Grill over hot coals 10 minutes or until scallops are opaque, turning and basting once with mustard mixture. Serve warm.

Makes 4 servings

Prep Time: 15 minutes
Cook Time: 10 minutes

Blackened Sea Bass

BACON–WRAPPED SHRIMP

**1 pound fresh or frozen large raw shrimp,
    shelled and deveined**
1 small onion, finely chopped
½ cup olive oil
½ teaspoon sugar
½ teaspoon garlic powder
½ teaspoon ground red pepper
¼ teaspoon salt
¼ teaspoon dried oregano leaves, crushed
½ pound bacon
Mexican Fried Rice (recipe follows)

Thaw shrimp, if frozen. For marinade, in small
bowl, combine onion, oil, sugar, garlic powder, red
pepper, salt and oregano. Place shrimp in large
resealable plastic food bag; set bag in deep bowl.
Pour marinade over shrimp in bag; seal bag.
Marinate shrimp 3 hours in refrigerator or 1 hour
at room temperature, turning occasionally.

Halve bacon slices lengthwise and crosswise. In
large skillet, partially cook bacon. Drain on paper
towels. Drain shrimp; discard marinade. Wrap
bacon strips around shrimp; secure with wooden
toothpicks. Place wrapped shrimp in wire grill
basket or on 12×9-inch piece of heavy-duty
aluminum foil. (If using foil, puncture foil in
several places.)

Grill shrimp on uncovered grill directly over
medium-hot KINGSFORD® Briquets 12 minutes
or until bacon is done and shrimp are opaque,
turning basket or individual shrimp once. Serve
with Mexican Fried Rice.   *Makes 6 servings*

Mexican Fried Rice

3 tablespoons vegetable oil
1 cup long-grain rice
**1 (8-ounce) package frozen raw shrimp,
    shelled and deveined (optional)**
1 cup salsa
½ cup chopped green bell pepper
1 small onion, chopped
1 clove garlic, minced

Heat oil in large skillet over medium heat. Add
rice; cook until golden brown, stirring frequently.
Stir in shrimp, salsa, bell pepper, onion, garlic and
2 cups water. Bring mixture to a boil; reduce heat
to low. Cover; simmer 15 to 20 minutes or until
rice is tender. Season to taste; serve with additional
salsa, if desired.   *Makes 6 servings*

SEAFOOD FAVORITES

CATFISH WITH FRESH CORN RELISH

4 catfish fillets (each about 6 ounces and at least ½ inch thick)
2 tablespoons paprika
½ teaspoon ground red pepper
½ teaspoon salt
Fresh Corn Relish (recipe follows)
Lime wedges
Grilled baking potatoes (optional)
Tarragon sprigs for garnish

Rinse fish; pat dry with paper towels. Combine paprika, red pepper and salt in cup; lightly sprinkle on both sides of fish.

Oil hot grid to help prevent sticking. Grill fish, on covered grill, over medium KINGSFORD® Briquets, 5 to 9 minutes. Halfway through cooking time, turn fish over and continue grilling until fish turns from translucent to opaque throughout. (Grilling time depends on thickness of fish; allow 3 to 5 minutes for each ½ inch of thickness.) Serve with Fresh Corn Relish, lime wedges and potatoes, if desired. Garnish with tarragon sprigs.

Makes 4 servings

Fresh Corn Relish

¼ cup cooked fresh corn or thawed frozen corn
¼ cup finely diced green bell pepper
¼ cup finely slivered red onion
1 tablespoon vegetable oil
2 tablespoons seasoned (sweet) rice vinegar
Salt and black pepper
½ cup cherry tomatoes, cut into quarters

Toss together corn, green pepper, onion, oil and vinegar in medium bowl. Season with salt and pepper. Cover and refrigerate until ready to serve. Just before serving, gently mix in tomatoes.

Makes about 1½ cups

SEAFOOD KABOBS

Nonstick cooking spray
1 pound raw large shrimp, peeled, deveined
10 ounces skinless swordfish or halibut
steaks, cut 1 inch thick
2 tablespoons honey mustard
2 teaspoons fresh lemon juice
8 metal skewers (12 inches long)
8 slices bacon (regular slice, not thick)
Lemon wedges (optional)

1. Spray room temperature barbecue grid with nonstick cooking spray. Prepare grill.

2. Place shrimp in shallow glass dish. Cut swordfish into 1-inch cubes on cutting board; add to shrimp in dish.

3. Combine honey mustard and lemon juice in small bowl. Pour over shrimp mixture; toss lightly to coat.

4. To assemble skewers, pierce skewer through 1 end of bacon slice. Add 1 piece shrimp. Pierce skewer through bacon slice again, wrapping bacon slice around 1 side of shrimp.

5. Add 1 piece swordfish. Pierce bacon slice again, wrapping bacon around opposite side of swordfish. Continue adding seafood and wrapping with bacon, pushing ingredients to middle of skewer until end of bacon slice is reached. Repeat with remaining skewers. Brush any remaining mustard mixture over skewers.

6. Place skewers on grid. Grill skewers, on covered grill, over medium coals 8 to 10 minutes or until shrimp are opaque and swordfish flakes easily when tested with fork, turning halfway through grilling time. Serve with lemon wedges.

Makes 4 servings (2 kabobs per serving)

NOTE: Kabobs can be prepared up to 3 hours before grilling. Cover and refrigerate until ready to grill.

GRILLED FRESH FISH

3 to 3½ pounds fresh tuna or catfish
¾ cup prepared HIDDEN VALLEY RANCH®
Original Ranch® Salad Dressing
Chopped fresh dill
Lemon wedges (optional)

Place fish on heavy-duty foil. Cover with salad dressing. Grill over medium-hot coals until fish turns opaque and flakes easily when tested with fork, 20 to 30 minutes. Or broil fish 15 to 20 minutes. Sprinkle with dill; garnish with lemon wedges, if desired.

Makes 6 servings

Seafood Kabobs

SEAFOOD FAVORITES

SNAPPER WITH PESTO BUTTER

½ cup butter or margarine, softened
1 cup packed fresh basil leaves, coarsely chopped *or* ½ cup chopped fresh parsley plus 2 tablespoons dried basil leaves, crushed
3 tablespoons finely grated fresh Parmesan cheese
1 clove garlic, minced
Olive oil
2 to 3 teaspoons lemon juice
4 to 6 red snapper, rock cod, salmon or other medium-firm fish fillets (at least ½ inch thick)
Salt and black pepper
Lemon wedges
Fresh basil or parsley sprigs and lemon strips for garnish

To make Pesto Butter, place butter, basil, cheese, garlic and 1 tablespoon oil in blender or food processor; process until blended. Stir in lemon juice to taste. Rinse fish; pat dry with paper towels. Brush one side of fish lightly with oil; season with salt and pepper.

Oil hot grid to help prevent sticking. Grill fillets, oil sides down, on covered grill, over medium KINGSFORD® Briquets, 5 to 9 minutes. Halfway through cooking time, brush tops with oil; season with salt and pepper. Turn and continue grilling until fish turns opaque throughout. (Allow 3 to 5 minutes for each ½ inch of thickness.) Serve each fillet with spoonful of Pesto Butter and wedge of lemon. Garnish with basil sprigs and lemon strips.

Makes 4 to 6 servings

GRILLED RAINBOW TROUT IN FOIL WITH VEGETABLES

4 CLEAR SPRINGS® Brand Idaho Rainbow Trout Fillets (4 ounces each)
8 asparagus spears, cut into 1½-inch pieces
4 small new potatoes, cooked and sliced ¼ inch thick
2 small tomatoes, halved and sliced
⅓ cup chopped green onions
2 teaspoons chopped fresh basil or thyme leaves *or* ½ teaspoon dried basil or thyme leaves, crushed
Black pepper

Cut four 10-inch squares of aluminum foil. Place trout fillets, flesh side up, diagonally across center of each square. Top with vegetables, herbs and pepper. Fold edges of foil square together and seal to make packets. Place on grill, about 4 inches above hot coals. Grill 6 to 10 minutes or until trout turns opaque, turning packets halfway through cooking time. To serve, carefully peel back foil.

Makes 4 servings

Snapper with Pesto Butter

SEAFOOD FAVORITES

GRILLED SHRIMP CREOLE

1 can (15 to 16 ounces) red beans
½ cup olive oil, divided
3 tablespoons balsamic or red wine vinegar
3 cloves garlic, minced, divided
1½ pounds raw large shrimp, peeled and deveined
3 tablespoons all-purpose flour
1 medium green bell pepper, coarsely chopped
1 medium onion, coarsely chopped
2 ribs celery, sliced
1 can (28 ounces) tomatoes, undrained, coarsely chopped
1 bay leaf
1½ teaspoons dried thyme leaves, crushed
¾ teaspoon hot pepper sauce
1 cup uncooked white rice, preferably converted
1 can (about 14 ounces) chicken broth
Hinged grill basket *or* 6 metal skewers (12 inches long)
¼ cup chopped fresh parsley

1. Place beans in strainer. Rinse under cold running water; drain. Set aside.

2. Combine ¼ cup oil, vinegar and 1 clove garlic in small bowl. Pour over shrimp; toss lightly to coat. Cover; marinate in refrigerator at least 30 minutes or up to 8 hours, turning occasionally.

3. For tomato sauce, heat remaining ¼ cup oil in large skillet over medium heat. Stir in flour. Cook and stir until flour is dark golden brown, 10 to 12 minutes. Add bell pepper, onion, celery and remaining 2 cloves garlic; cook and stir 5 minutes. Add tomatoes with juice, bay leaf, thyme and hot pepper sauce. Simmer, uncovered, 25 to 30 minutes or until sauce has thickened and vegetables are fork-tender, stirring occasionally.*

4. Meanwhile, prepare grill. While coals are heating, prepare rice according to package directions, substituting broth for 1¾ cups water and omitting salt. Stir in beans during last 5 minutes of cooking.

5. Drain shrimp; discard marinade. Place shrimp in grill basket or thread onto skewers. Place grill basket or skewers on grid. Grill shrimp, on uncovered grill, over medium coals 6 to 8 minutes or until shrimp are opaque, turning halfway through grilling time.

6. Remove and discard bay leaf from tomato sauce. Arrange rice and beans on 4 serving plates; top with tomato sauce. Remove shrimp from grill basket or skewers. Arrange shrimp over tomato sauce. Sprinkle with parsley. *Makes 4 servings*

*If desired, tomato sauce may be prepared up to 1 day ahead. Cover and refrigerate. Reheat sauce in medium saucepan over medium heat while shrimp are grilling.

Grilled Shrimp Creole

SURF AND TURF BROCHETTES

1 (12-ounce) beef top round steak, cut into ¾-inch cubes
24 small shrimp, peeled and deveined
1 green bell pepper, cut into 1-inch squares
¾ cup orange juice
½ cup A.1.® Steak Sauce
2 tablespoons white wine
1 clove garlic, minced
1½ teaspoons cornstarch

Soak 12 (10-inch) wooden skewers in water for at least 30 minutes. Alternately thread beef cubes, shrimp and green pepper onto skewers.

In small saucepan, combine orange juice, steak sauce, wine and garlic; reserve ½ cup mixture for basting. Blend cornstarch into remaining steak sauce mixture in saucepan. Over medium heat, cook and stir until sauce thickens and begins to boil; keep warm.

Grill brochettes over medium heat for 8 to 10 minutes or until shrimp turn pink and opaque and beef is cooked, turning and brushing often with reserved steak sauce mixture. Serve brochettes with warm sauce for dipping. *Makes 12 appetizers*

BARBECUED SALMON

4 salmon steaks (at least ¾ inch thick)
3 tablespoons lemon juice
2 tablespoons soy sauce
Salt and black pepper
½ cup K.C. MASTERPIECE® Barbecue Sauce (about)

Rinse fish; pat dry with paper towels. Combine lemon juice and soy sauce in shallow glass dish. Place steaks in dish; let stand at cool room temperature no more than 15 to 20 minutes, turning steaks several times. Remove fish; discard marinade. Season lightly with salt and pepper.

Oil hot grid to help prevent sticking. Grill salmon, on covered grill, over medium KINGSFORD® Briquets, 10 to 14 minutes. Halfway through cooking time, brush top with barbecue sauce, then turn and continue grilling until fish turns from translucent to opaque throughout. (Grilling time depends on thickness of fish; allow 3 to 5 minutes for each ½ inch of thickness.) Remove fish from grill; brush with barbecue sauce.

Makes 4 servings

SEAFOOD FAVORITES

SHANGHAI FISH PACKETS

**4 orange roughy or tilefish fillets
(4 to 6 ounces each)**
¼ cup mirin* or Rhine wine
3 tablespoons soy sauce
1 tablespoon Oriental sesame oil
1½ teaspoons grated fresh ginger
¼ teaspoon crushed red pepper
1 tablespoon peanut or vegetable oil
1 clove garlic, minced
**1 package (10 ounces) fresh spinach leaves,
destemmed**

*Mirin is a Japanese sweet wine available in Japanese markets and the gourmet section of large supermarkets.

1. Prepare grill. Place orange roughy in single layer in large shallow dish. Combine mirin, soy sauce, sesame oil, ginger and crushed red pepper in small bowl; pour over orange roughy. Cover; marinate in refrigerator 20 minutes.

2. Heat peanut oil in large skillet over medium heat. Add garlic; cook and stir 1 minute. Add spinach; cook and stir until wilted, about 3 minutes, tossing with 2 wooden spoons.

3. Place spinach mixture in center of each of four 12-inch squares of heavy-duty foil. Remove orange roughy from marinade; reserve marinade. Place 1 orange roughy fillet over each mound of spinach. Drizzle reserved marinade evenly over orange roughy. Wrap in foil.

4. Place packets on grid. Grill packets, on covered grill, over medium coals 15 to 18 minutes or until orange roughy flakes easily when tested with fork.

Makes 4 servings

VEGETABLE–TOPPED FISH POUCHES

**4 firm fish fillets, such as flounder, cod or
halibut (about 1 pound)**
1 carrot, cut into very thin strips
1 rib celery, cut into very thin strips
1 medium red onion, cut into thin wedges
1 medium zucchini or yellow squash, sliced
8 mushrooms, sliced
**½ cup (about 2 ounces) shredded Swiss
cheese**
½ cup WISH-BONE® Italian Dressing*

*Also terrific with Wish-Bone® Robusto Italian or Lite Italian Dressing.

On four 18×9-inch pieces heavy-duty aluminum foil, divide fish equally. Evenly top with vegetables, then cheese, then Italian dressing. Wrap foil loosely around fillets and vegetables, sealing edges airtight with double fold. Let stand to marinate 15 minutes. Grill or broil pouches, seam sides up, 15 minutes or until fish flakes easily with fork.

Makes 4 servings

SUN–KISSED SHRIMP KABOBS

16 jumbo-size shrimp (about 1 pound)
⅓ cup KIKKOMAN® Teriyaki Marinade & Sauce
1 green onion and tops, minced
1 clove garlic, pressed
1 teaspoon grated lemon peel
½ teaspoon sugar
1 can (8 ounces) pineapple chunks in syrup, drained

Leaving shells on tails, peel shrimp; devein. Combine teriyaki sauce, green onion, garlic, lemon peel and sugar in medium bowl. Add shrimp; toss to coat well. Reserving teriyaki sauce mixture, remove shrimp and place 1 pineapple chunk in curve of each shrimp. Thread each of 4 (12-inch) metal or bamboo* skewers with 4 shrimp and pineapple. Place kabobs on grill 4 to 5 inches from hot coals; brush with reserved teriyaki sauce mixture. Cook 4 minutes; turn kabobs over. Brush with remaining teriyaki sauce mixture. Cook 3 minutes longer, or just until shrimp turn pink. (Or, place kabobs on rack of broiler pan 4 to 5 inches from heat. Brush with reserved teriyaki sauce mixture. Broil 4 minutes; turn over. Brush with remaining teriyaki sauce mixture. Broil 4 minutes longer, or until shrimp turn pink.)

Makes 4 servings

*Soak bamboo skewers in water 30 minutes to prevent burning.

TERIYAKI TROUT

4 whole trout (about 2 pounds)
¾ cup LAWRY'S® Teriyaki Marinade with Pineapple Juice, divided
½ cup sliced green onions
2 medium lemons, sliced
Chopped fresh parsley (optional)

Pierce skin of trout several times with fork. Brush inside and outside of each trout with Teriyaki Marinade with Pineapple Juice; stuff with green onions and lemon slices. Place in shallow glass dish. Pour all but ¼ cup Teriyaki Marinade with Pineapple Juice over trout; cover dish. Marinate in refrigerator at least 30 minutes. Heat grill for medium-hot coals. Remove trout, reserving marinade. Place trout in oiled hinged wire grill basket; brush with reserved marinade. Grill, 4 to 5 inches from heat source, 10 minutes or until trout flakes easily when tested with fork, turning and brushing occasionally with reserved ¼ cup Teriyaki Marinade with Pineapple Juice. Sprinkle with parsley, if desired. *Makes 4 servings*

PRESENTATION: For a delicious side dish, cook sliced bell pepper, onion and zucchini brushed with vegetable oil on grill with trout.

Sun-Kissed Shrimp Kabobs

SALADS & SIDES

BARBECUED CORN WITH THREE SAVORY BUTTERS

12 ears corn, unhusked
Three Savory Butters (recipes page 98)

Carefully peel back husks; remove corn silk. Bring husks up and tie securely with kitchen string. Soak corn in cold water to cover 30 minutes.

Place corn on grid. Grill over medium-high coals 25 minutes or until corn is tender, turning often. Remove string and husks. Serve with your choice of savory butter.

Makes 12 side-dish servings

Prep Time: 40 minutes
Cook Time: 25 minutes

(continued on page 98)

SALADS & SIDES

(Three Savory Butters, continued from page 96)

Horseradish Butter
  ½ cup (1 stick) butter or margarine, softened
  3 tablespoons FRENCH'S® Bold'n Spicy® Mustard
  1 tablespoon horseradish

RedHot® Chili Butter
  ½ cup (1 stick) butter or margarine, softened
  2 tablespoons FRANK'S® Original REDHOT® Cayenne Pepper Sauce
  1 teaspoon chili powder
  1 clove garlic, minced

Herb Butter
  ½ cup (1 stick) butter or margarine, softened
  2 tablespoons snipped fresh chives
  1 tablespoon FRENCH'S® Worcestershire Sauce
  1 tablespoon minced fresh parsley
  ½ teaspoon dried thyme leaves
  ½ teaspoon salt (optional)

Place ingredients for each flavored butter in separate small bowls; beat until smooth. Serve at room temperature.   *Makes about ½ cup each*

TIP: Try Deep South BBQ Sauce on ribs. Combine ½ cup *each* ketchup and molasses, ¼ cup *each* FRENCH'S® Worcestershire Sauce and FRENCH'S® Classic Yellow® Mustard, and ½ teaspoon hickory salt. Brush on ribs during last 10 minutes of grilling. Serve with corn for a great meal.

GRILLED BEEF SALAD

  ½ cup mayonnaise
  2 tablespoons cider vinegar or white wine vinegar
  1 tablespoon spicy brown mustard
  2 cloves garlic, minced
  ½ teaspoon sugar
  6 cups torn assorted greens such as romaine, red leaf and Bibb, destemmed
  1 large tomato, seeded and chopped
  ⅓ cup thinly sliced fresh basil leaves
  1 small red onion, sliced
  1 pound boneless beef top sirloin steak, cut 1 inch thick
  ½ teaspoon salt
  ½ teaspoon pepper
  ½ cup purchased herb or garlic croutons
  Additional pepper (optional)

Prepare grill. Combine mayonnaise, vinegar, mustard, garlic and sugar in small bowl; mix well. Cover; refrigerate until serving. Toss together greens, tomato, basil and onion rings in large bowl; cover and refrigerate until serving.

Sprinkle both sides of steak with salt and ½ teaspoon pepper. Place steak on grid. Grill steak, on covered grill, over medium-hot coals 10 minutes for medium-rare, turning halfway through grilling time. Transfer steak to carving board. Slice in half lengthwise; carve crosswise into thin slices. Add steak and croutons to greens; toss well. Add mayonnaise mixture; toss until well coated. Serve with additional pepper.   *Makes 4 servings*

Grilled Beef Salad

SALADS & SIDES

GRILLED ANTIPASTO

⅔ cup A.1.® Steak Sauce
¼ cup lemon juice
2 tablespoons olive oil
1 teaspoon dried basil leaves
2 cloves garlic, minced
16 medium scallops (about ⅔ pound)
16 medium shrimp, shelled and deveined (about ¾ pound)
12 mushrooms
2 ounces thinly sliced cooked roast beef or ham
16 (2×½-inch) eggplant strips
1 (6½-ounce) jar marinated artichoke hearts, drained
1 red bell pepper, thickly sliced
Lettuce leaves and lemon wedges, for garnish

Soak 12 (10-inch) wooden skewers in water for at least 30 minutes. In medium bowl, combine steak sauce, lemon juice, olive oil, basil and garlic; set aside.

Thread 4 scallops onto each of 4 skewers and 4 shrimp onto each of 4 skewers; thread 6 mushrooms onto each of 2 skewers. Cut roast beef or ham into 3×1-inch strips; wrap around eggplant strips and secure with wooden toothpicks. Wrap remaining beef or ham around artichoke hearts; thread onto remaining 2 skewers. Place skewers, eggplant bundles and pepper slices on baking sheet; brush with steak sauce mixture.

Grill over medium heat for 7 to 10 minutes or until seafood is opaque and vegetables are tender, turning and basting several times. Remove each item from grill as it is done; place on large lettuce-lined serving platter. Serve garnished with lemon wedges, if desired.   *Makes 8 appetizer servings*

SAVORY GRILLED POTATOES IN FOIL

½ cup MIRACLE WHIP® Salad Dressing
3 garlic cloves, minced
½ teaspoon paprika
¼ teaspoon salt
¼ teaspoon pepper
3 baking potatoes, cut into ¼-inch slices
1 large onion, sliced

• Mix salad dressing and seasonings in large bowl until well blended. Stir in potatoes and onion to coat.

• Divide potato mixture evenly among six 12-inch square pieces of heavy-duty foil. Seal each to form packet.

• Place foil packets on grill over medium-hot coals (coals will have slight glow). Grill, covered, 25 to 30 minutes or until potatoes are tender.

Makes 6 side-dish servings

Prep Time: 15 minutes
Grill Time: 30 minutes

Grilled Antipasto

SALADS & SIDES

SOUTH–OF–THE–BORDER VEGETABLE KABOBS

 5 cloves garlic, peeled
½ cup A.1.® BOLD Steak Sauce
¼ cup FLEISCHMANN'S® Margarine, melted
 1 tablespoon finely chopped cilantro
¾ teaspoon ground cumin
¼ teaspoon coarsely ground black pepper
⅛ teaspoon ground red pepper
 3 ears corn, cut crosswise into 1½-inch-thick slices and blanched
 3 medium plum tomatoes, cut into ½-inch-thick slices
 1 small zucchini, cut lengthwise into thin slices
 1 cup baby carrots, blanched

Mince 1 garlic clove; halve remaining garlic cloves and set aside. In small bowl, combine steak sauce, margarine, cilantro, minced garlic, cumin and peppers; set aside.

Alternately thread vegetables and halved garlic cloves onto 6 (10-inch) metal skewers. Grill kabobs over medium heat for 7 to 9 minutes or until vegetables are tender, turning and basting often with steak sauce mixture. Remove from skewers; serve immediately.   *Makes 6 servings*

SAVORY ONION GLAZED FOCACCIA

½ cup finely chopped onion
 3 cloves garlic, minced
¼ cup olive oil
 3 tablespoons A.1.® Steak Sauce
 1 (10-ounce) can refrigerated pizza crust dough
 3 tablespoons finely chopped parsley
 3 tablespoons finely chopped sun-dried tomato
 1 teaspoon dried oregano leaves
½ teaspoon coarsely ground black pepper

In small skillet, over medium heat, sauté onion and garlic in 2 tablespoons oil until tender; remove from heat. Stir in steak sauce; set aside.

Unroll dough and flatten slightly; brush one side of dough with 1 tablespoon oil. Grill dough, oil side down, over low heat for 3 to 4 minutes or until dough is firm and brown. Brush top of dough with remaining tablespoon oil and turn over on grill surface. Top evenly with steak sauce mixture, parsley, tomato, oregano and pepper. Grill 4 to 5 minutes or until bottom is golden; serve hot.

Makes 6 servings

SALADS & SIDES

GRILLED VEGETABLE AND RAVIOLI SALAD

**1 package (9 ounces) CONTADINA®
Refrigerated Fat Free Garden Vegetable
Ravioli, cooked and drained**
**1 pound assorted fresh vegetables, such as
zucchini, onion, eggplant, red, yellow or
green bell peppers, grilled and diced**
**1 cup lightly packed, torn assorted salad
greens**
**1⅔ cups (12-ounce container) CONTADINA®
Refrigerated Light Garden Vegetable
Sauce**
2 tablespoons olive oil
2 tablespoons red wine vinegar

In medium bowl, combine ravioli, vegetables and
salad greens. In small bowl, combine garden
vegetable sauce, oil and vinegar; mix well. Add to
pasta; toss well. Serve immediately.

Makes 4 servings

SWEET & SOUR SLAW

**1 can (29 ounces) cling peach halves in
syrup, undrained**
⅓ cup mayonnaise
1 tablespoon KIKKOMAN® Soy Sauce
1 tablespoon vinegar
¼ teaspoon ground ginger
¼ teaspoon minced garlic
3 hard-cooked eggs
1 quart shredded cabbage*
Paprika (optional)

*If using both red and green cabbage, shred 1 small
head of each.

Reserving syrup, drain peaches; set aside. Blend
reserved peach syrup with mayonnaise, soy sauce,
vinegar, ginger and garlic; set aside. Quarter 2
eggs; remove yolks. Press yolks and remaining
whole egg through sieve. Combine sieved eggs
with 2 tablespoons mayonnaise mixture; spoon
mixture into quartered egg whites. Drizzle peach
halves with part of remaining mayonnaise mixture.
Add remaining mayonnaise mixture to cabbage in
large bowl; toss lightly to coat. To serve, divide
slaw into 4 individual salad bowls; place 2 peach
halves, cut side up, in each bowl. Place 1 filled egg
quarter in each peach half. Garnish with paprika, if
desired. *Makes 4 servings*

SALADS & SIDES

GRILLED TRI-COLORED PEPPER SALAD

1 each large red, yellow and green bell pepper, cut into halves or quarters
⅓ cup extra-virgin olive oil
3 tablespoons balsamic vinegar
2 cloves garlic, minced
¼ teaspoon salt
¼ teaspoon black pepper
⅓ cup crumbled goat cheese (about 1½ ounces)
¼ cup thinly sliced fresh basil leaves

Prepare grill. Place bell peppers, skin side down, on grid. Grill bell peppers, on covered grill, over hot coals 10 to 12 minutes or until skin is charred. Place charred bell peppers in paper bag. Close bag; set aside to cool 10 to 15 minutes. Remove skin with paring knife; discard skin.

Place bell peppers in shallow glass serving dish. Combine oil, vinegar, garlic, salt and black pepper in small bowl; whisk until well combined. Pour over bell peppers. Let stand 30 minutes at room temperature. (Or, cover and refrigerate up to 24 hours. Bring bell peppers to room temperature before serving.) Sprinkle bell peppers with cheese and basil just before serving.

Makes 4 to 6 servings

GRILLED CORN-ON-THE-COB

¼ pound butter or margarine, softened
1 tablespoon KIKKOMAN® Soy Sauce
½ teaspoon dried tarragon leaves, crumbled
6 ears fresh corn

Thoroughly blend butter, soy sauce and tarragon leaves. Husk corn. Lay each ear on piece of foil large enough to wrap around it; spread ears generously with seasoned butter. Wrap foil around corn; seal edges. Place on grill 3 inches from hot coals; cook 20 to 30 minutes, or until corn is tender, turning over frequently. (Or, place wrapped corn on baking sheet. Bake at 325°F, 30 minutes.) Serve immediately. *Makes 6 side-dish servings*

KIKKO-STYLE FRENCH ROLLS

4 tablespoons butter or margarine
1 tablespoon KIKKOMAN® Teriyaki Marinade & Sauce
¼ teaspoon garlic powder
4 French rolls

Combine butter, teriyaki sauce and garlic powder in small saucepan with heatproof handle; heat on grill until butter melts. Slice each roll in half lengthwise. Place rolls, cut side down, on grill 3 to 4 inches from hot coals; cook about 2 minutes, or until golden brown. Brush butter mixture equally on each toasted roll half. *Makes 4 servings*

Grilled Tri-Colored Pepper Salad

SALADS & SIDES

GRILLED CAJUN POTATO WEDGES

3 large russet potatoes, washed and scrubbed (do not peel) (about 2¼ pounds)
¼ cup olive oil
2 cloves garlic, minced
1 teaspoon salt
1 teaspoon paprika
½ teaspoon dried thyme leaves, crushed
½ teaspoon dried oregano leaves, crushed
¼ teaspoon black pepper
⅛ to ¼ teaspoon ground red pepper
2 cups mesquite chips

1. Prepare grill. Preheat oven to 425°F.

2. Cut potatoes in half lengthwise, then cut each half lengthwise into 4 wedges. Place potatoes in large bowl. Add oil and garlic; toss to coat well.

3. Combine salt, paprika, thyme, oregano, black pepper and ground red pepper in small bowl. Sprinkle over potatoes; toss to coat well. Place potato wedges in single layer in shallow roasting pan. (Reserve remaining oil mixture left in large bowl.) Bake 20 minutes.

4. Meanwhile, cover mesquite chips with cold water; soak 20 minutes. Drain mesquite chips; sprinkle over coals. Place potato wedges on their sides on grid. Grill potato wedges, on covered grill, over medium coals 15 to 20 minutes or until

potatoes are browned and fork-tender, brushing with reserved oil mixture halfway through grilling time and turning once with tongs.

Makes 4 to 6 servings

GRILLED CORN SOUP

4 ears Grilled Corn-on-the-Cob (recipe follows)
5 green onions
4 cups chicken broth, divided
Salt and black pepper

Cut kernels from cobs to make 2 to 2½ cups. Slice green onions, separating the white part from the green. Place corn, white part of onions and 2 cups chicken broth in blender or food processor; process until mixture is slightly lumpy. Place corn mixture in large saucepan; add remaining chicken broth. Simmer gently 15 minutes. Stir in sliced green onion tops; season to taste with salt and pepper.

Makes 4 to 6 servings

GRILLED CORN-ON-THE-COB: Turn back corn husks; *do not remove.* Remove silks with stiff brush; rinse corn under cold running water. Smooth husks back into position. Grill ears, on a covered grill, over medium-hot KINGSFORD® Briquets, about 25 minutes or until tender, turning corn often. Remove husks and serve.

Grilled Cajun Potato Wedges

SALADS & SIDES

HERBED MUSHROOM VEGETABLE MEDLEY

4 ounces button or crimini mushrooms
1 medium red or yellow bell pepper, cut into ¼-inch-wide strips
1 medium zucchini, cut crosswise into ¼-inch-thick slices
1 medium yellow squash, cut crosswise into ¼-inch-thick slices
3 tablespoons butter or margarine, melted
1 tablespoon chopped fresh thyme leaves *or* 1 teaspoon dried thyme leaves, crushed
1 tablespoon chopped fresh basil leaves *or* 1 teaspoon dried basil leaves, crushed
1 tablespoon chopped fresh chives or green onion tops
1 clove garlic, minced
¼ teaspoon salt
¼ teaspoon black pepper

Prepare grill. Cut thin slice from base of mushroom stems with paring knife; discard. Thinly slice mushroom stems and caps. Combine mushrooms, bell pepper, zucchini and squash in large bowl. Combine butter, thyme, basil, chives, garlic, salt and black pepper in small bowl. Pour over vegetable mixture; toss to coat well.

Transfer mixture to 20×14-inch sheet of heavy-duty foil; wrap. Place foil packet on grid. Grill packet, on covered grill, over medium coals 20 to 25 minutes or until vegetables are fork-tender. Open packet carefully to serve.

Makes 4 to 6 servings

GRILLED SWEET POTATO PACKETS WITH PECAN BUTTER

4 sweet potatoes (about 8 ounces each), peeled and cut into ¼-inch-thick slices
1 large sweet or Spanish onion, thinly sliced and separated into rings
3 tablespoons vegetable oil
⅓ cup butter or margarine, softened
2 tablespoons packed light brown sugar
¼ teaspoon salt
¼ teaspoon ground cinnamon
¼ cup chopped pecans, toasted

Prepare grill. Alternately place potato slices and onion rings on four 14×12-inch sheets of heavy-duty foil. Brush tops and sides with oil to prevent drying. Wrap in foil. Place foil packets on grid. Grill packets, on covered grill, over medium coals 25 to 30 minutes or until potatoes are fork-tender.

Meanwhile, to prepare Pecan Butter, combine butter, sugar, salt and cinnamon in small bowl; mix well. Stir in pecans. Open packets carefully; top each with dollop of Pecan Butter.

Makes 4 servings

Herbed Mushroom Vegetable Medley

SALADS & SIDES

GRILLED FRUIT KABOBS

⅓ **cup dairy sour cream**
⅓ **cup apricot preserves**
¼ **cup A.1.® Steak Sauce**
1½ **cups pineapple chunks (fresh or canned)**
1 **cup seedless grapes**
1 **orange, sectioned**
1 **large banana, cut into 12 chunks**
1 **tablespoon FLEISCHMANN'S® Margarine, melted**

Soak 12 (10-inch) wooden skewers in water for at least 30 minutes. In small bowl, combine sour cream, apricot preserves and 1 tablespoon steak sauce; set aside.

Thread fruit pieces onto skewers. In small bowl, combine remaining 3 tablespoons steak sauce with melted margarine; brush kabobs with margarine mixture. Grill fruit over medium heat for 5 minutes or until warm and very lightly browned, turning and basting with remaining margarine mixture. Serve warm with sour cream sauce for dipping. *Makes 12 appetizers*

GRILLED PASTA SALAD

4 **medium zucchini and/or yellow squash, sliced**
1 **medium Spanish onion, halved and cut into large chunks**
1 **envelope LIPTON® Recipe Secrets® Savory Herb with Garlic Soup Mix**
¼ **cup olive or vegetable oil**
8 **ounces penne, rotini or ziti pasta, cooked and drained**
¾ **cup diced roasted red peppers**
¼ **cup red wine vinegar, apple cider vinegar or white vinegar**

• Also terrific with Lipton® Recipe Secrets® Italian Herb with Tomato or Golden Onion Soup Mix.

On heavy-duty aluminum foil, arrange zucchini and onion. Brush with savory herb with garlic soup mix blended with oil. Grill or broil 5 minutes or until golden brown and crisp-tender.

In large bowl, toss cooked pasta, vegetables, roasted peppers and vinegar. Serve warm or at room temperature.
Makes about 4 main-dish or 8 side-dish servings

Grilled Fruit Kabobs

SAUCES & MARINADES

PINEAPPLE SALSA

1 can (20 ounces) DOLE® Crushed
    Pineapple, drained
½ cup finely chopped DOLE® Red Bell
    Pepper
¼ cup finely chopped DOLE® Green Bell
    Pepper
1 tablespoon chopped DOLE® Green Onion
2 teaspoons chopped fresh cilantro or
    parsley
2 teaspoons finely chopped jalapeño
    peppers
1 teaspoon grated lime peel

- Combine ingredients in small bowl.

- Serve salsa at room temperature or slightly chilled over grilled chicken or fish.

Makes 8 servings

Prep Time: 20 minutes

SAUCES & MARINADES

BACON & ONION RELISH

½ pound sliced bacon, cut into small pieces
2 large yellow onions, thinly sliced
2 tablespoons red wine vinegar
Salt and black pepper

Cook bacon in medium skillet over low heat until almost crisp. Drain off drippings. Add onions; cook and stir over medium heat until golden brown. Stir in vinegar; season with salt and pepper to taste. Serve hot. Refrigerate leftovers.

Makes 1 cup

SERVING SUGGESTION: Serve as a topping for grilled BOB EVANS FARMS® Sandwich Patties on a bun.

SWEET & SOUR RELISH

1 medium onion, chopped
1 stalk celery, chopped
½ cup prepared chili sauce
2 tablespoons dark brown sugar
2 tablespoons cider vinegar
Dash dried tarragon leaves

Combine ingredients in medium saucepan. Bring to a boil over medium-high heat. Reduce heat to low; simmer 5 minutes, stirring occasionally. Serve hot or cold. Refrigerate leftovers and reheat if necessary.

Makes 1 cup

SERVING SUGGESTION: Serve with grilled BOB EVANS FARMS® Bratwurst, Smoked Sausage or Kielbasa.

GAZPACHO RELISH

4 teaspoons tomato paste
2 teaspoons red wine vinegar
2 teaspoons lime juice
1½ teaspoons olive oil
½ pound tomatoes, peeled, seeded and chopped
¼ cup minced green bell pepper
¼ cup peeled and chopped cucumber
4 canned artichoke hearts, chopped
2 teaspoons minced shallots
2 teaspoons chopped fresh dill
¼ teaspoon black pepper
3 to 6 drops hot pepper sauce

Place tomato paste, vinegar, juice and oil in blender or food processor; process until smooth. Transfer mixture to medium bowl and stir in remaining ingredients. Cover and refrigerate several hours before serving. Serve cold. Refrigerate leftovers.

Makes 1 cup

SERVING SUGGESTION: Serve as an accompaniment to grilled BOB EVANS FARMS® Sandwich Patties or chicken.

From top: Bacon & Onion Relish, Sweet & Sour Relish and Gazpacho Relish

SAUCES & MARINADES

MEXICAN HAMBURGER TOPPING

½ cup HELLMANN'S® or BEST FOODS® Real or Light Mayonnaise or Low Fat Mayonnaise Dressing
½ cup prepared chunky salsa, drained
½ cup (2 ounces) shredded Cheddar cheese
½ cup refried beans

In small bowl combine mayonnaise, salsa, cheese and beans. Serve with hamburgers.

Makes about 1⅔ cups

BACON HAMBURGER TOPPING: Combine 1 cup mayonnaise and ¼ cup crumbled cooked bacon or real bacon bits. *Makes about 1 cup*

GREEN ONION HAMBURGER TOPPING: Combine 1 cup mayonnaise and ¼ cup sliced green onions. *Makes about 1 cup*

K.C. MASTERPIECE® SPREAD

¼ cup K.C. MASTERPIECE® Barbecue Sauce
¼ cup reduced-calorie or regular mayonnaise

Combine barbecue sauce and mayonnaise in small bowl until smooth. Serve with grilled beef, turkey, chicken or pork. *Makes ½ cup*

JAMAICAN BBQ SAUCE

⅓ cup molasses
⅓ cup prepared mustard
⅓ cup red wine vinegar
3 tablespoons Worcestershire sauce
¾ teaspoon TABASCO® pepper sauce

Combine ingredients in small bowl until well blended. Use as a baste while grilling beef, chicken, pork or game. *Makes 1 cup*

***From top:** Bacon Hamburger Topping, Mexican Hamburger Topping and Green Onion Hamburger Topping*

HONEY STRAWBERRY SALSA

1½ cups diced sweet red pepper
1 cup sliced fresh strawberries
1 cup diced green bell pepper
1 cup diced fresh tomato
⅓ cup honey
¼ cup chopped Anaheim pepper
¼ cup lemon juice
2 tablespoons finely chopped fresh cilantro
1 tablespoon tequila (optional)
½ teaspoon crushed dried red chili pepper
½ teaspoon salt
¼ teaspoon pepper

Combine ingredients in glass container; mix well. Cover tightly and refrigerate overnight to allow flavors to blend. Serve on grilled fish or chicken.

Makes 3 to 4 cups

Favorite recipe from **National Honey Board**

HONEY BARBECUE SAUCE

1 can (10¾ ounces) condensed tomato soup
½ cup honey
2 to 3 tablespoons vegetable oil
2 tablespoons Worcestershire sauce
1 tablespoon lemon juice
1 teaspoon prepared mustard
Dash ground red pepper or bottled hot pepper sauce (optional)

Combine ingredients in medium saucepan. Bring to a boil over medium heat. Reduce heat to low and simmer, uncovered, 5 minutes. Use as a baste while grilling beef, ribs or poultry.

Makes about 2 cups

Favorite recipe from **National Honey Board**

HERBED HONEY LIME SAUCE

½ cup minced onion
1 tablespoon olive oil
1 cup dry white wine or chicken broth
¼ cup honey
¼ cup lime juice
2 teaspoons dry mustard
1 teaspoon minced fresh rosemary
½ teaspoon salt
Dash pepper
1 teaspoon cornstarch
1 teaspoon water

Cook and stir onion in olive oil in medium saucepan over medium heat until onion is softened. Stir in wine, honey, lime juice, mustard, rosemary, salt and pepper; mix well and bring to a boil. Combine cornstarch and water in small bowl or cup, mixing well; add to sauce. Cook over low heat, stirring until sauce comes to a boil and thickens. Serve over cooked turkey, chicken, fish or pork.

Makes 2 cups

Favorite recipe from **National Honey Board**

From top: Honey Barbecue Sauce, Honey Strawberry Salsa and Herbed Honey Lime Sauce

BARBECUED GARLIC

8 whole heads fresh garlic*
¼ cup butter or margarine, melted
4 sprigs fresh rosemary or oregano *or*
     2 teaspoons dried rosemary or oregano
     leaves, crushed

*The whole garlic bulb is called a head.

Preheat grill. Peel outer skin layers of garlic, leaving cloves and head intact. Place heads on double thickness of foil; drizzle with butter and sprinkle with herbs. Fold up foil, leaving space around edges and crimping all ends to make packet. Place packet on grid. Grill over hot coals 40 to 45 minutes, turning occasionally. Serve 1 whole head per person. Squeeze cooked cloves from skin onto cooked meat and vegetables or spread on French or rye bread.

Makes 8 servings

Favorite recipe from **Christopher Ranch Garlic**

TERIYAKI MARINADE

½ cup A.1.® Steak Sauce
¼ cup teriyaki sauce
2 tablespoons Dijon mustard

In small nonmetal bowl, combine steak sauce, teriyaki sauce and mustard. Use to marinate beef, fish steaks, poultry or pork for about 1 hour in refrigerator.

Makes ¾ cup

TANGY LEMON GLAZE

½ cup apple juice
¼ cup firmly packed brown sugar
½ cup A.1.® Steak Sauce
2 tablespoons lemon juice
1 tablespoon cornstarch
1 teaspoon grated lemon peel

In small saucepan, blend apple juice and brown sugar. Stir in steak sauce, lemon juice, cornstarch and lemon peel. Over medium heat, heat to a boil, stirring constantly. Boil 1 minute; remove from heat and cool slightly. Use as a baste while grilling poultry, pork or ham.

Makes about 1¼ cups

SAUCES & MARINADES

SWEET 'N' SASSY BBQ SAUCE

2 tablespoons corn oil
1 large onion, chopped
1 can (15 ounces) tomato sauce
¾ cup sugar
⅓ cup FRANK'S® Original REDHOT®
    Cayenne Pepper Sauce
¼ cup FRENCH'S® Worcestershire Sauce
½ teaspoon ground allspice

Heat oil in medium saucepan over medium-high heat. Add onion; cook and stir until tender. Add remaining ingredients. Bring to a boil. Reduce heat to medium-low. Cook, uncovered, 20 minutes or until thickened, stirring often. Baste on grilled chicken or ribs during last 10 minutes of cooking. Refrigerate any leftover sauce or serve as a dipping sauce. *Makes 2½ cups*

Prep Time: 5 minutes
Cook Time: 25 minutes

ZIPPY TARTAR SAUCE FOR GRILLED FISH

1 cup mayonnaise
3 tablespoons FRANK'S® Original REDHOT®
    Cayenne Pepper Sauce
2 tablespoons FRENCH'S® Bold'n Spicy®
    Mustard
2 tablespoons sweet pickle relish
1 tablespoon minced drained capers

Combine mayonnaise, RedHot® sauce, mustard, pickle relish and capers in medium bowl; mix well. Cover and refrigerate until ready to serve. Serve with grilled salmon or halibut. *Makes 1½ cups*

Prep Time: 5 minutes

RED RELISH

1 red bell pepper, quartered and seeded
1 large tomato, cut into halves, seeded and
    squeezed to drain some juice
2 tablespoons balsamic vinegar*
2 tablespoons chopped fresh basil
Salt and black pepper to taste

*Substitute 1 tablespoon red wine vinegar plus ½ teaspoon sugar for the balsamic vinegar.

Grill red pepper, skin side down, on uncovered grill, over medium KINGSFORD® Briquets, until skin starts to blister and pepper turns limp. Add tomato to grill 2 minutes after pepper. Grill until tomato begins to turn limp. Remove from grill and let cool. Chop pepper and tomato; combine with remaining ingredients. Serve with grilled beef, turkey, chicken, pork or fish.

Makes about 1⅓ cups

THAI MARINADE

½ cup A.1.® Steak Sauce
⅓ cup peanut butter
2 tablespoons soy sauce

In small nonmetal bowl, combine steak sauce, peanut butter and soy sauce. Use to marinate beef, poultry or pork for about 1 hour in refrigerator.

Makes 1 cup

HONEY BASTING SAUCE

¾ cup A.1.® Steak Sauce
2 tablespoons honey
2 tablespoons dry sherry
1 teaspoon cornstarch
¼ teaspoon dried basil leaves

In small saucepan, blend steak sauce, honey, sherry, cornstarch and basil. Over medium heat, heat to a boil, stirring constantly. Boil 1 minute; remove from heat and cool slightly. Use as a baste while grilling beef, poultry or pork.   *Makes about 1 cup*

NEW MEXICO MARINADE

1½ cups beer
½ cup chopped fresh cilantro
3 cloves garlic
½ cup lime juice
2 teaspoons chili powder
1½ teaspoons ground cumin
1 teaspoon TABASCO® pepper sauce

Place ingredients in food processor or blender; process until well combined. Store in 1-pint covered jar in refrigerator up to 3 days. Use to marinate beef, pork or chicken in refrigerator.

Makes 2 cups

ITALIAN MARINADE

1 envelope GOOD SEASONS® Italian, Zesty Italian or Garlic & Herb Salad Dressing Mix
⅓ cup oil
⅓ cup dry white wine or water
2 tablespoons lemon juice

Mix salad dressing mix, oil, wine and lemon juice in cruet or medium bowl until well blended. Reserve ¼ cup marinade for basting; refrigerate. Pour remaining marinade over 1½ to 2 pounds meat, poultry or seafood. Toss to coat well; cover. Refrigerate to marinate. Drain before grilling.

Makes ⅔ cup

Thai Marinade

——Acknowledgments——

The publisher would like to thank the companies and organizations listed below for the use of their recipes and photographs in this publication.

American Lamb Council

Best Foods, a Division of
    CPC International Inc.

Bob Evans Farms®

California Beef Council

Christopher Ranch Garlic

Clear Springs Foods

Dole Food Company, Inc.

Delmarva Poultry Industry, Inc.

Del Monte Foods

Holland House, a division of
    Cadbury Beverages Inc.

The HVR Company

Kikkoman International Inc.

The Kingsford Products Company

Kraft Foods, Inc.

Lawry's® Foods, Inc.

Thomas J. Lipton Co.

McIlhenny Company

Nabisco, Inc.

National Broiler Council

National Cattlemen's Beef Association

National Honey Board

National Pork Producers Council

Nestlé Food Company

Perdue® Farms

Reckitt & Colman Inc.

USA Rice Council

—Index—

METRIC CONVERSION CHART

VOLUME MEASUREMENTS (dry)

$\frac{1}{8}$ teaspoon = 0.5 mL
$\frac{1}{4}$ teaspoon = 1 mL
$\frac{1}{2}$ teaspoon = 2 mL
$\frac{3}{4}$ teaspoon = 4 mL
1 teaspoon = 5 mL
1 tablespoon = 15 mL
2 tablespoons = 30 mL
$\frac{1}{4}$ cup = 60 mL
$\frac{1}{3}$ cup = 75 mL
$\frac{1}{2}$ cup = 125 mL
$\frac{2}{3}$ cup = 150 mL
$\frac{3}{4}$ cup = 175 mL
1 cup = 250 mL
2 cups = 1 pint = 500 mL
3 cups = 750 mL
4 cups = 1 quart = 1 L

VOLUME MEASUREMENTS (fluid)

1 fluid ounce (2 tablespoons) = 30 mL
4 fluid ounces ($\frac{1}{2}$ cup) = 125 mL
8 fluid ounces (1 cup) = 250 mL
12 fluid ounces (1$\frac{1}{2}$ cups) = 375 mL
16 fluid ounces (2 cups) = 500 mL

WEIGHTS (mass)

$\frac{1}{2}$ ounce = 15 g
1 ounce = 30 g
3 ounces = 90 g
4 ounces = 120 g
8 ounces = 225 g
10 ounces = 285 g
12 ounces = 360 g
16 ounces = 1 pound = 450 g

DIMENSIONS

$\frac{1}{16}$ inch = 2 mm
$\frac{1}{8}$ inch = 3 mm
$\frac{1}{4}$ inch = 6 mm
$\frac{1}{2}$ inch = 1.5 cm
$\frac{3}{4}$ inch = 2 cm
1 inch = 2.5 cm

OVEN TEMPERATURES

250°F = 120°C
275°F = 140°C
300°F = 150°C
325°F = 160°C
350°F = 180°C
375°F = 190°C
400°F = 200°C
425°F = 220°C
450°F = 230°C

BAKING PAN SIZES

Utensil	Size in Inches/Quarts	Metric Volume	Size in Centimeters
Baking or	8×8×2	2 L	20×20×5
Cake Pan	9×9×2	2.5 L	22×22×5
(square or	12×8×2	3 L	30×20×5
rectangular)	13×9×2	3.5 L	33×23×5
Loaf Pan	8×4×3	1.5 L	20×10×7
	9×5×3	2 L	23×13×7
Round Layer	8×1½	1.2 L	20×4
Cake Pan	9×1½	1.5 L	23×4
Pie Plate	8×1¼	750 mL	20×3
	9×1¼	1 L	23×3
Baking Dish	1 quart	1 L	—
or Casserole	1½ quart	1.5 L	—
	2 quart	2 L	—